C0-AVH-895

# Teaching What Can't Be Taught

## The Shaman's Strategy

David Rigoni

A SCARECROWEDUCATION BOOK

The Scarecrow Press, Inc.
Lanham, Maryland, and London
2002

040952 7

A SCARECROWEDUCATION BOOK

Published in the United States of America
by Scarecrow Press, Inc.
A Member of the Rowman & Littlefield Publishing Group
4720 Boston Way, Lanham, Maryland 20706
www.scarecroweducation.com

PO Box 317 Oxford
OX2 9RU, UK

Copyright © 2002 by David Rigoni

*All rights reserved.* No part of this publication may be reproduced,
stored in a retrieval system, or transmitted in any form or by any
means, electronic, mechanical, photocopying, recording, or otherwise,
without the prior permission of the publisher.

British Library Cataloguing in Publication Information Available

**Library of Congress Cataloging-in-Publication Data**
Rigoni, David, 1947–
  Teaching what can't be taught : the shaman's strategy / David Rigoni.
    p. cm.
Includes bibliographical references and index.
  ISBN 0-8108-4362-5 (hard : alk. paper)—ISBN 0-8108-4361-7 (pbk. : alk.
paper)
  1. Learning. 2. Teaching. 3. Problem solving. I. Title.
  LB1060 .R54 2002
  370.15'23—dc21                                            2002004526

∞™  The paper used in this publication meets the minimum requirements of
American National Standard for Information Sciences—Permanence of Paper
for Printed Library Materials, ANSI/NISO Z39.48-1992.
Manufactured in the United States of America.

To three people who have always provided their unconditional love, support, and encouragement: my wife, Pat, and my parents, Mary and Chris Rigoni.

# Contents

0409527

# Figures

# Preface

This book is not intended as a manual to produce New Age shamans or to proliferate ethereal New Age philosophies. There is no call for drum beating or chanting, spirit-guides, or excursions to an underworld. Instead, the focus of this book is to offer a different view of education than we tend to hold in our current time and culture. It is about how we learn the important things that are not (in fact, *cannot*) be explicitly taught in formal situations.

So why use a shaman metaphor? This book argues that the most important part of any education involves between-the-lines learning that changes a student's world view. The connection with shamanic practice is a natural one, as the fundamental focus of a shaman's teaching involves purposefully changing the world view of an apprentice. What separates a shaman from an ordinary teacher is that a shaman is conscious and intentional in effecting that world view change. The world view changes that do occur in most contemporary educational settings tend to be accidental (or at least incidental), while rapt attention is afforded the means to that end.

This book, then, uses a shaman-as-teacher metaphor to argue that what is (at worst) absent or (at best) implicit and unconscious in contemporary education needs to be made explicit and conscious, and what is currently thought to be an end product is, in actuality, merely an intermediate step to an elusive end.

# Acknowledgments

I wish to acknowledge my "Ideal Readers" who provided encouragement, who helped me "murder my darlings," and who were responsible for many substantive changes in this manuscript. Thanks to: William Rigoni, Clark Whiting, Carol Koch, Dr. Susan Huber, Dr. Trudi Taylor, and Mary Gliniany.

Special thanks Dr. Donald LaMagdeleine from the University of St. Thomas, whose fingerprints are all over this manuscript.

I also wish to acknowledge some of my shaman-teachers, who probably were unaware that they left fingerprints all over my life: Miss Brezinski and Mr. Kowolski (teachers didn't have first names back then) from South Milwaukee High School. Dr. James Mehoke, Mr. Loren Browning, Dr. Thomas Sheehan, and Mrs. Katherine Davis from the University of Wisconsin–Superior. Dr. Stephen Preskill from the University of St. Thomas.

# Chapter One

# A Path with Heart

For me there is only the traveling on paths that have a heart, on any path
that may have a heart. There I travel, and the only worthwhile challenge
is to traverse its full length. And there I travel, looking, looking breath-
lessly. —Don Juan

> Carlos Castaneda, *The Teachings of Don Juan: A Yaqui Way of*
> *Knowledge* (New York: Ballantine Books, 1968), xii.

Many years ago, I read a poster that declared, "Life is a journey, not a des-
tination." That poster struck a chord in me, as I had just begun a journey
looking for answers to questions about my own learning. The path I set off
on has taken many twists, turns, and detours, and my search has expanded
over the years to questions about how people learn the important things in
a culture in which the less important things are increasingly valued. This
book is a report on my journey.

The essential questions about my own learning burst into my consciousness years ago as a result of a particular event. It was an incident
that I remember vividly even today. I remember walking nervously down
the long, sterile hallway of the public university I was attending. The hallway was painted that institutional beige so popular in public buildings.
The heavy, dark wood doors were all closed because professors were seldom in their offices. When they were, students bombarded them with
questions, so they simply stayed away. The doors held notices of office
hours that were never kept and brief notes to students, such as "Pascal assignments not graded yet—check back Tuesday." Now, at the end of the

semester, final grades, identified by social security numbers, were also taped to doors. The federal government hadn't yet declared that practice illegal.

I walked nervously, fearing what I was about to discover. I was a high school English teacher at the time, suffering from something that would later be named burnout. Depressed at the thought of reading yet another student paper crammed with sentence fragments and comma splices, I was exploring a professional change. The computer profession was gaining visibility and popularity; mainframe computers were increasingly popular, and newly invented microcomputers were emerging as a technological force.

I had just completed a course called Assembly Language Programming. I had done very well in my first computer courses, but this one was different. This was an intense programming course placed at this juncture in the curriculum to weed out the faint of heart and (I feared) people with backgrounds in English rather than mathematics. This had been the accelerated summer version of the course, covering all seventeen text chapters in six weeks. The course details had been mired in an incoherent muck of too much in too short a time. I had dreamt the unsettling dreams of a bewildered student, working feverishly in my sleep to decipher long printouts of binary and octal code "dumps." The class had weeded out students with considerable proficiency. Of the sixty-plus students who had begun this course, fewer than half had attended the last class. Of that thirty, about half had shown up for the final.

The class had presented new challenges for me. I would feel as though I had grasped my studies well until I would take a test; then I would stare at the test questions as if they had been written in some alien language. When my test was returned, I would mumble the mantra of contemporary students to anyone who would listen: "I knew the material better than this; I guess I'm just not good at taking tests." I had known that I wasn't being totally truthful, even to myself. Now I was about to find out how I had done on the final exam and in the course. I was not optimistic.

I was relieved to see that the door of my course instructor (Dr. Irving) was closed; I couldn't bear the thought of looking at him that day. I ran my finger down the left column of the page taped to his door, found my social security number, then traced it across the line to the right column to find my grade. My heart sank. I had received a D. I had feared it. In a way,

I had expected it. But also, in that uniquely human way, I really hadn't believed it would happen. I was smart; I was an adult; I was a teacher. Right? I already had a college degree. Right? So how could I receive a D? I had sat through the class until the end; I had worked hard on the assignments; I was part of the 25 percent who had taken the final . . . and I had just received my first university D.

I thought about this class and Dr. Irving for the rest of the summer as I questioned my fitness for this profession. Dr. Irving was actually an excellent classroom teacher. He was organized and methodical, and he explained topics well. It was outside the classroom where a tension existed between us. I was first introduced to Dr. Irving by my friend, John, a high school mathematics teacher. Irving was cordial enough that first time, but I was aware that his expression became curious when I told him that I taught high school English.

I'm sure I quickly confirmed his expectation that I was not going to be his star student; I suspect he believed I had no business being in his program. I remember to this day the cold, harsh stare of Irving's steel-gray eyes when I would stop by his office to ask him a question; I remember how he would sit back in his chair, scarcely examining my printouts, irritated with me for bothering him, a Brahmin avoiding the contamination of an untouchable. He reacted differently to my friend, John. When John asked a question, the coldness left Irving's eyes, his voice acquired a friendlier tone, and he leaned forward to examine John's printouts. John was a good student; he was part of the fraternity; he spoke the language of mathematics. I wondered: was it true that most students simply were not cut out to be computer scientists? Would only a particularly dim-witted English major intentionally wander into this hostile territory?

In the end, I stubbornly decided not to accept Irving's verdict. That fall, I took the course a second time from a different professor, a man who, in contrast to Irving, was one of the most incompetent professors ever to occupy a classroom. In the interim, something had happened to me, something had "clicked." This time, I barely opened my text. I breezed through the assignments. I understood the material well enough to follow the haphazard mumblings of my pathetic new professor. This time, I received one of the handful of A's in the class.

I realized, in fairness to Irving, that I had understood the content of the course well enough the first time, but I hadn't understood how to think like a computer scientist. Years later, a frustrated student would ask me, "Is it okay if we just memorize this stuff instead of understand it?" In retrospect, I understood that I had merely memorized the material; I hadn't understood it. Understanding came abruptly, early in the second course, when the perspective shifted, suddenly becoming simple and apparent. Irving hadn't arbitrarily assigned me a D; he had merely evaluated my progress to that point. I hadn't understood the material in Irving's class as well as I wanted to believe I had. I could see that now. Somehow since then, I had received a Zen-like vision of the obvious; I had achieved understanding and clarity. I recognized the assumptions that accompanied a computer problem; I could see the art and style in its solution. This was a critical experience for me, and I was immediately intrigued with how this happened so suddenly and so completely.

Thereafter, I was a "successful" computer student. I seemed to have found the mystical key to the esoteric nature of computer work. I learned new things quickly. Many other things I simply knew without studying them. I'm sure Dr. Irving would have been stunned to learn that I eventually moved on to become a computer professor myself. One of my first students, after spending a summer working for a large computer company, asked me a question upon his fall return to campus. He said, "I'm curious. You were totally accurate about how computer things are done in industry. How did you know this stuff when you never worked in industry?" The only answer I had was that I had my key. There is a consistent, internal viewpoint to the profession. Anyone who has the key to that viewpoint can accurately gauge most practices that derive from it.

After years of teaching in a computer department myself, I came to better understand Irving's perspective that not everyone was suited to be a computer professional. But I came to resent that perspective as well. Was he only willing to help those who didn't need help? Were there only certain people who were supposed to be successful in this profession? Was there anything he could have done to help me learn what I needed earlier and easier? Had he given up on me too soon? I tried to use Irving and my own experiences as a touchstone to keep my perspectives of my own students honest. I knew from experience that professors can judge students incorrectly; I knew that some students who seemed hopeless at one checkpoint might find the key by the next. I also knew that some remained hopeless.

A second pivotal experience further influenced my explorations. Although my first experience brought the problem into my consciousness, the second experience helped me to focus and refine that problem. The experience involved a course I proudly taught called Introduction to Problem Solving. This was an elective class that former students often touted as a vital milestone in their progression toward successful computer careers. Students told their peers, "You have to take this class; I don't know what I would have done without it." One student told me that the course so dramatically changed her approach to problem solving in her personal life that even her husband had commented on it.

This particular year, my Problem Solving class was a debacle. My students were nice people; they were attentive in class and seemed to work hard on assignments—but sometimes in the midst of apparent understanding, they would suddenly seem dazed and confused. Sometimes even the simplest problems bewildered and frustrated them. The line outside my office often resembled holiday commuter lines at an airport. One tutoring session with Jodie stands out in my mind. Jodie was an obviously intelligent woman in her late teens who had sole responsibility for her daughter; she was under considerable financial stress and felt the dilemma of trying to balance her new roles of college student and parent. In some respects, this session was an archetypal representation of many others; yet, it stands out for me because of the obvious pain this class was causing this student.

The problem on which the class had been working was an hourly-rate payroll problem, a problem assigned by every computer teacher since the dawn of digital time. The essence of the problem involves determining whether or not an employee has worked any overtime (e.g., hours over forty), and calculating the person's pay with one formula if there is overtime, with a different formula if there is not. Jodie stopped by for help with this problem.

She showed me a lot of incoherent scribblings that indicated to me that she didn't know where to begin. She was trying, but she was lost. We had struggled to work through the problem in different ways for a few minutes when it became clear to me that she was having problems with a basic programming structure called an IF-ELSE statement. This type of statement tests a condition, the result of which will be either true or false; if it is true, the program branches to one set of statements; if it is false, it branches to a different set. I decided to explain it with a non-computer example, as students often understood it better that way.

"If it rains tomorrow, we will cancel class; otherwise, we won't," I said. "Let's break that statement into its three parts. What is the condition we are testing?"

"If it rains tomorrow," she answered with certainty.

"Right. What is the 'true' action; what will we do if it rains tomorrow?"

"Cancel class?" she answered hesitantly.

"Good. Then what is the 'false' action; what will we do if it does anything except rain tomorrow?"

"Have class." She was surer of herself. There was only one option left.

"Now," I continued, "let's look at the payroll problem. What is the question we need to ask?"

She shrugged her shoulders. She looked as though she probably couldn't answer without breaking into tears.

"What are the two types of data we're being given?" I retreated to a consideration we had already discussed.

She answered slowly with a question. "Hours and pay rate?"

"Now, considering that this is an overtime problem, which one of the two data elements do we need to form into a condition to test?"

"Pay rate?" she answered, again with a question. (This is obviously the wrong answer, as the problem involves overtime hours and as the hours, not the pay rate, will change from week to week.)

My own frustration level was growing, frustration with myself for not being able to get her to see the obvious answer, and with her for not being able to see it. My face evidently showed it.

"I can see that you're getting frustrated," she said. "I don't blame you— you've been so patient with me. I'll just look at it some more at home."

I assured her that I was only upset with myself, but I was not convincing. We tried a few more tactics, but we both knew that it was only to help both of us save face. We both wondered if it was true that some people simply don't "get" this stuff.

I felt shamed, saddened, and humbled after this session and others like it. I felt shamed that I couldn't hide my frustration; I felt saddened that I couldn't help my students understand. I also felt humbled that I knew so little about the teaching/learning process. As a result of this class, I knew

I needed to reconsider how learning actually took place and to how I as a teacher could facilitate that process. I was consumed with questions. How could I help my students see the obvious solutions to simple problems? Why did some strategies work for past classes but not this one? Was something different with this class or with me? The full realization of the staggering complexity of the teaching/learning process crashed down on me.

My first experience of getting a D, retaking the course, and getting an A had impacted the kind of teacher I now tried to be. I tried to reserve judgment, be patient, and give students time to master their studies. I attempted to emulate the best aspects of Dr. Irving and to remedy his shortcomings. When students seemed to be struggling, I would tell them that although it was possible that they should choose a different discipline, it was also possible that they just needed to give it more time. Sometimes they were successful, and sometimes they were not and changed majors. But it hadn't occurred to me yet to investigate this on a deeper level.

My experience with the disastrous Problem Solving class made me realize that being understanding about my students' difficulties and frustrations did not always help them to learn what they needed to learn or to be less frustrated when they didn't learn it. My approach didn't address the fact that some students learned what they needed to learn, and some students didn't, in fact, *couldn't*. It was after "teaching" this class that I knew I needed to find out more.

*Chapter Two*

# Knee-Deep in Quantum Foam, Searching for a Place to Stand

When a man starts to learn, he is never clear about his objectives. His purpose is faulty; his intent is vague. He hopes for rewards that will never materialize, for he knows nothing of the hardships of learning.

He slowly begins to learn—bit by bit at first, then in big chunks. And his thoughts soon clash. What he learns is never what he pictured, or imagined, and so he begins to be afraid. Learning is never what one expects. —Don Juan

> Carlos Castaneda, *The Teachings of Don Juan: A Yaqui Way of Knowledge* (New York: Ballantine Books, 1968), 79.

This quotation is a stunning statement about learning. What we customarily call teaching and learning in our society is essentially just the transmission and storage of facts. Real learning is more dramatic and more unpredictable. It isn't linear. It isn't neat and orderly. And it is dangerous. It is dangerous because it changes the way we see things; it causes us to view the world through uncomfortable new lenses. I became acutely aware of this process as I continued my search, as my own learning reflected Don Juan's words. The answers didn't line up like schoolchildren preparing for recess. Instead, key thoughts and key thinkers trickled in randomly, sporadically. Some thinkers led me sideways or backward to other thinkers who had influenced them. Some books jumped off of shelves into my hands; some were handed to me by friends and colleagues; some I tripped over while looking for others. The results took me in directions and changed me in ways I could never have anticipated.

This all occurred over a number of years. Certain thinkers eventually joined together with other thinkers like pieces in a puzzle. I began to envision the jigsaw puzzles of my youth, laid out on card tables with some sections filling in beautifully alongside stacks of individual pieces that I was certain would never fit anywhere, pieces that were obviously included in the puzzle box by mistake. Eventually, the key thinkers provided enough substance and language to give me rudimentary ways of describing the learning I was investigating, and other pieces filled in neatly around these.

Puzzle pieces emerged from ideas in the fields of anthropology, sociology, quantum physics, and philosophy, which examined learning as a social process. This was intriguing to me, as the theoretical base of most teacher preparation programs consists of developmental and educational psychology, which treat learning as a series of isolated, individual events based primarily on the readiness and the internal psyche of a person. Instead, the emerging ideas implied that although learning is individually constructed, it is an intensely creative, social act.

## SEEKING A PLACE TO STAND

This chapter examines a lot of ideas and theories—answers to my questions could not be explored without my examining them. However, because this book is being written primarily for practitioners, and because practitioners have tended to dislike (and distrust) theory, I need to take what Madeleine Hunter (of Direct Instruction fame) would have called a bird walk. To her, a bird walk was something a teacher wanted to say that contributed minimally to the actual goal of a lesson. I have personally found bird walks to be incredibly valuable and powerful. Students I have encountered years after having had them in class have remembered the bird walks long after the lessons have been forgotten. So I'd like to step off the path momentarily and consider the importance of grounding theory to the practice of our profession.

Donald Schön depicts us humans as living in a techno-rational cultural paradigm. One of the main attributes of such a paradigm is that we are essentially unaware of its existence or its rules. To someone living in a given culture, paradigm rules are simply "the way things are" or "the way things are done." It is for this reason that we are not aware of such things as our own spoken dialects. We don't notice a dialect unless it is different from our own, and anyone who doesn't share our dialect "talks funny." A cultural paradigm requires that someone point out to us what we probably wouldn't notice otherwise. It is like moving to another region and discovering that *we* not only "talk funny" but "think funny" as well. Schön performs such a service for us by making us aware that our invisible techno-rational culture routinely splits into dichotomies things that ought not be split.

Two of the dichotomies he identifies, separation of research from practice and separation of knowing from doing,[1] especially concern us here. Once split, research and knowing are afforded higher status than practice and doing. The division of theory (i.e., research) and practice, especially, has deep cultural roots. American educators, because we are not separate from our culture(s), tend to cooperate fully in this polarization. By training, by cultural acquisition, and even by inherent tendencies that lure an individual into a particular profession, most K–12 practitioners dutifully abhor theory and most university academics respectfully worship at its feet.

Although there are exceptions, it is possible to draw some generalities about this dichotomy. At one extreme of the continuum, we find theorists (researchers) who often ignore and denigrate practice. It is their job to think deep thoughts; it is for other (lesser) individuals to put these deep thoughts to (lesser) practical use. These people believe theory is much more important than practice, and, not surprisingly, believe theorists are much more important than practitioners. At the other extreme of the continuum, we find practitioners who often ignore and denigrate theory. It is their job to *do* things in life; it is for individuals incapable of actually doing anything to think up theories that have no real-life application. Only things that can be used in class tomorrow are important. These people believe that practice is more important than theory, and, not surprisingly, that practitioners are more important than theorists.

Over the years, I have witnessed both ends of this continuum. As a student observing friends, I have watched eyes immediately glaze over and brains beam out to favorite vacation spots the instant an instructor introduced any theoretical considerations. As an instructor observing peer performance, I have watched colleagues lecture from a distant theoretical planet, oblivious to the needs of students sitting in front of them. Each group has what the other lacks and lacks what the other has. To theorize without considering practical implications is arrogant and elitist; to practice without considering theoretical foundations is negligent and shortsighted. An exclusive dependence on either theory or practice is problematic. A position of balance at the center of the continuum is ideal. Although theory without application is as problematic as its evil twin, change will be slow here, as things change ever so slowly in academia. It might be noted that we still wear medieval robes at formal academic events. Years ago, I came across this quotation (source unknown) attributed to physicist Max Planck:

> A new scientific truth does not triumph by convincing its opponents and making them see the light. But, rather, because its opponents eventually die and a new generation grows up that is familiar with it.

I expect the reunion of theory with practice will require the same process in academia. Academics (especially in large universities) are systematically rewarded for being theoretical. Those who tentatively venture into the area of practice (through applied research or good teaching) often pay a professional price for their cultural deviance, often failing to receive tenure, promotion, and credibility. Mirroring the dichotomy of the larger society outlined by Schön, a tension exists in universities between many liberal arts and professional faculties; the former deal primarily with theory, and the latter, while dabbling in foundational theory, concentrate on practice.

Even in smaller universities, where a pleasant face is generally put on it, this tension exists in subtle but real ways. I recently witnessed a small "turf" issue that illustrates this point. Although nonacademics might expect more lofty behavior from people who (with polysyllabic words, strident voices, and much arm waving) espouse the value of broadening our perspectives, most disagreements in academia are narrow (often petty) turf/status issues. No turf/status issue is too trivial to escape academic attention or to evoke brushfire outrage. This one involved the lofty matter of which major should be listed first on a student transcript. A liberal arts faculty member declared that an "academic" major should always be listed on a transcript before a "professional" major; in the event that there are two academic majors, those majors should be listed alphabetically but still always before the professional major.

No reason was given. To the speaker, the reason was self-evident — traditional academic majors are simply more important and authentic than contemporary professional majors. After being confronted by a professional program faculty member, the academic person quickly declared that he had not intended to insult professional programs; he was, in fact, supportive of them. He simply felt that the logic was obvious, and he apologized for any "misunderstanding" of what he said. In academic-speak, such phrasing is less an apology than an expression of civility intended to avoid further hostility with another who is incapable of understanding a self-evident point. He did not apologize for what he actually said, or what he actually thought about the issue. With the salve of misunderstanding spread over the wound, life continued exactly as it had before this enlightening exchange, with the liberal arts faculty member left scratching his head, wondering what all the fuss was about. This faculty member (arguably an intelligent and honorable man) continued to perpetuate a false dichotomy through a paradigm of which he remained blissfully unaware.

I expect the second-tier status of practice in theory-loving universities to continue well into the future. But as there is at least talk of change these days, there is some hope even if the reward systems do not yet reinforce this talk. I also expect I will have a better chance of making a case for enticing some practitioners to integrate a theoretical perspective into their practice. This, too, will be difficult, but it is easier in a sense. Most practitioners don't reject theory out of hand in the same way many academics reject practice. Rather, they avoid theory for other reasons. First, they have been told repeatedly that they have no use for theory. Second, they have been told repeatedly that they are not good at theory and shouldn't attempt it. This makes practitioners reluctant to utilize theory and afraid to "play" with it. In both cases, practitioners are listening to people who often have a vested interest in keeping theory to themselves. In our techno-rational society, those with the theory get the power, respect, and financial rewards; those who have only practice do not.

I know of one elementary school principal who didn't want his faculty taking a summer enrichment class to discuss literary theory because such thinking would "just make them dissatisfied when they return to their classrooms in the fall." He was obviously concerned that if his teachers grew and changed, it would needlessly complicate his life. Others want practitioners to uncritically accept the theories they want to sell. Such vendors denigrate theory and offer their materials as the exclusive "practical" answer. Two examples from Lee Canter in defense of his Assertive

Discipline classroom management approach demonstrate this point. The first quotation is from the Canter and Canter textbook; it bemoans the fact that

> exposure to so many different philosophies has resulted in the fact that there is no longer "one way" to run a classroom and teach students.[2]

This is an excellent marketing line that resonates with many practitioners. It says essentially: *We feel your pain. We understand just how complicated your job is, how unappreciated you feel, and how confusing you find all this theoretical talk. Teachers used to just teach, and now it's so complicated and everyone is questioning what you're doing. Don't listen to all that—we have the answers, simple answers. Don't listen to them. You can follow our cookbook approach without all that confusing theory stuff; don't worry your pretty little heads about all that—we've taken care of it for you.*

Defending Assertive Discipline in a publication, Canter plays more directly to the perceived biases of his audience. Using good marketing sound bites, he is again saying theory isn't important; teachers shouldn't be concerned with theory—just follow our program; we've taken care of all that for you.

> Theories . . . make interesting reading, but teachers don't need more educational literature. They need answers, and they need them now.[3]

In this second example, Canter is simply reinforcing messages to a target audience that had accepted these "truths" long before Canter had suggested them. Theory has no practical application to your practice, he is saying, and you don't have time to think about it anyway. It has always been curious to me that more teachers don't find such statements insulting. The message is, leave theory to the trained professionals; don't attempt this at home on your own.

There are two overriding arguments for practitioners to consider theory. The first is that all practice *already has* foundational theory beneath it. There is no such thing as theoryless practice. The only real question is whether or not someone is willing to acknowledge and examine that theory. When we practice without understanding the theory that supports it, we are essentially saying, "I'm just going to it this way; I really don't know (or care) why." Of course, the problem with this is that we may actually be utilizing practices contrary to our espoused teaching philosophies.

We human beings are adroit at placing our ideas and actions into discrete compartments, like dinner on partitioned cafeteria trays, ensuring that our food never touches. We believe in strict, conservative laws that ought never apply to our own families. We believe that government should stay out of our businesses and lives but call upon it to levy protectionist tariffs and to prevent election recounts. We have fervent religious beliefs that we fail to extend to our business or personal lives. A colleague of mine recently had some teachers in her graduate class bemoan student absenteeism in their schools prior to informing her that they would miss the next two weeks of her weekly class—without seeing a connection.

To ignore theoretical considerations is to ignore our compartments. I have a personal example. I once wrote a reflection paper for a graduate class that stated my views on a topic and went on to explore the topic in the theoretical terms we were discussing in this class. To my shock, by the time I got to the conclusion of my paper, I held exactly the opposite opinion I had stated in my introduction. This demonstrated to me the power of examining theory. My original belief had been held in isolation from other considerations. After looking at that belief in a broader theoretical context, I now needed to adjust the belief to fit my larger views on education. Theory reduces the isolation of our compartments and forces us to revise either our practice or our theoretical roots.

For example, many public school teachers assume they can mix and match pieces of different classroom management programs. I am aware of many who wish to unite favorite aspects of both Canter and Glasser. However, when examined from a theoretical perspective, the stimulus-response theory of Canter is diametrically opposed to the control theory of Glasser. The joined aspects will fight against each other and the combined approach will either be clunky or fail altogether. Theory is nothing more than the unstated assumptions behind our practice—we simply cannot have an integrated, consistent practice without considering what our practice implies beneath the surface. The bottom line is, theory is simply the thinking and beliefs that go into our practice. Our practice is the *what* and the *how*. Theory is the *why*.

The second overriding reason to consider theory will become clearer later in this chapter. In short, maybe *theory* is a value-loaded word. What we are talking about is simply a way of looking at the world. People who chafe at the notion of theory are essentially irritated by the notion of examining the context of their lives and actions. We tend to believe we are emancipated agents, free of outside influence, acting on our own volition, when in fact we are playing out roles bounded by our historical ways of looking at the world. Often called a paradigm or a world view, a theory influences how we look at the world. In fact, it may be that it determines how we *create* the world. It determines what we see and how we deal with it. To ignore theory is to limit what we see and to limit the options available in interacting with what we see. This is, in fact, a key idea I've come across on my journey. It will take several pages to make this complex set of ideas clear.

Archimedes had said, "Give me a long enough lever and a place to stand, and I will move the earth." That's what we are seeking here. We are not just babbling about meaningless theory or impractical ideas. We are seeking a place to stand, a place solid enough to support other ideas we may have, a place that will not collapse or cave in when we stack other ideas on top of it. It is the lack of a place to stand that causes so much of our contemporary malaise.

## DON'T CHOKE ON TOO MUCH THEORY

This chapter and the next cover two different levels of theory. This chapter covers the "deep" theory, the ideas the furthest from practice, the basic concepts that underlie everything else. The next chapter covers "surface" theory, which more directly relates to the practice of teaching. For readers with a theoretical inclination, I do recommend a careful reading of both chapters in order to completely understand the entire argument. However, if playing with theory is new for you, you may want to take it slowly. Trying to swallow the whole theoretical picture at once might make you choke and decide never to venture in this direction again. If that happens, I have done you a great disservice.

Theory is like exercise; you need to ease your way into it to be successful and to find it helpful. When initial exercise is overdone, you get sore and stop exercising. So here is what I recommend: read on in this chapter for a while. See if anything in it makes any impression on you. Some items will seem totally disconnected as I lay out information and return to it using stories to help place it in a context. *But*, when you feel yourself disconnecting from it, when your mind starts to wander, when it just begins to feel like a lot of work, when you start wondering if I'm ever going to get to the important stuff—stop. Live to exercise another day. When that happens, you've reached your limit.

If you decide you've had enough of this chapter, jump ahead to the next chapter. It still deals with theory, but it leads more directly into the practice of teaching. If you do this, you will still understand most of my argument. It will be akin to watching a movie made from a novel. If you see a movie with a friend who has read the book, you will both understand the movie, but your friend (who is aware of characterization and plot subtleties) will simply understand it a little better than you. You can always read the book after seeing the movie, and you can always return to the theory after reading about its implications.

## BELIEVING IS SEEING

People rarely understand or even notice great historical transitions as they take place; it is said that Louis XVI, at the end of the day the Bastille fell, wrote in his diary, Rien, "Nothing happened." Revolutions of belief are even more elusive, because they take place within human minds. You don't always know what's going on, even when it is your own mind that has been the scene of the upheaval.

Walter Truett Anderson, "Four Different Ways to Be Absolutely Right," in *The Truth about the Truth*, ed. Walter Truett Anderson (New York: Tarcher Putnam, 1995), 113–114.

## Prevailing Paradigms

The huge contribution of the social sciences has been to make us aware that we live our lives within cultural paradigms unique to our particular historical and geographical positioning in the world. A paradigm is a world view that is so much a part of us and that we take so totally for granted that it is invisible to us in our everyday lives. A paradigm is dynamic and grows out of changing social thought patterns, and it grows into an impressive force that in turn influences the thinking from which it emerged. A paradigm influences, even dictates, the way we view every single thing in our worlds. Although we live within multiple large and small paradigms, those I will be discussing in this section are the major paradigms of Western civilization. Academics differ somewhat on their delineation of these major paradigms; it is a pie that can be cut different ways. For the purposes of our discussion, I will label the categories as premodern, modern, and postmodern (see figure 2.1).

The premodern is sometimes subdivided further into the ancient and the medieval paradigms. The ancient one was characterized particularly by the Greeks and, later, the mimicking Romans. Influential remnants of Greek philosophy, drama, and mythology remain today. Plato and Aristotle are still fundamental elements of philosophical and theological education, and physicians still take the Hippocratic oath. The Romans appropriated essential elements of the Greek culture, and today the names of the Roman gods are assigned to planets in our solar system, and the medical field still uses Latin as its official language. This illustrates the continuity and leakage between paradigms. A paradigm always builds upon some elements of the previous paradigm and discards other elements. The medieval paradigm, on the other hand, was a para-

| | Premodern | Modern | Postmodern |
|---|---|---|---|
| **Truth** | Truth revealed | Truth discovered | Truth created |
| **Inquiry** | Astrology and religious revelation | Quantitative methods: replication and statistics | Qualitative methods: ethnography, case studies, etc. |
| **World View** | Humankind as center of creation | Machine-like universe; determinism | Randomness; probability |
| **Values** | Status quo; acquiescence to fixed reality | Progress through control and modification of fixed reality | Diversity; acceptance of alternative viewpoints |
| **Reality/ Knowledge** | Reality is real | Reality is a representation | Reality is a social construction |
| **Authority** | Church/clerics | Science/professions | Individuals/groups |
| **Education** | Tutoring; apprenticeship | Standardization; replication | Individualization; local uniqueness |

Figure 2.1   Major Western World Views

digm of Catholic Christianity. Truth was centralized in the hierarchy of the Catholic Church and in civil royalty. This was an autocratic paradigm in which truth was revealed through faith in scripture and the teachings of the church. Truth flowed directly from God to the church to individuals.

The modern paradigm signaled the end of the autocracy of the medieval period. It was marked by the rise of science. This paradigm also marked the beginning of establishing secular truth through scientific method rather than the dictates of church hierarchies. Rationality became more important than faith. Several scientific discoveries were fundamental in eroding the medieval view of ourselves during this period. Copernicus removed the Earth as the center of creation when he proclaimed that the Earth revolved around the sun rather than the entire universe revolving around the Earth. Darwin removed humans as the central focus of a special act of creation, reducing them to simply another mammal emerging from the primordial slime. And Freud further removed individuals as spiritual creations when he depicted unconscious, irrational inner drives within individuals. Today we live in a world that takes for granted our position as an infinitesimal speck in a vast universe, the theory of evolution, and Freud's ideas about our inner motivations.

One possible reason that our current age produces so much personal anxiety is that we are living with a minimum of three conflicting paradigms with roots simultaneously in the premodern, the modern, and the postmodern. This causes inevitable, unexamined anxiety, since the three world views oppose each other in critical ways, creating conflicting social perceptions and expectations. Thus, our foundations are never secure, and we can't ever be sure about which reality rules to access and implement. Two quick stories will illustrate paradigms in action.

Not long ago, I was seated in a dentist's chair, making small talk with a dental assistant who felt compelled to chat with me while we waited for the dentist. She asked, "What do you do?" In our culture, this question meant she was asking about my occupation. I answered, "I'm a teacher." She said, "Oh." (Not terribly impressed.) The next cultural question: "Where do you teach?" I told her the name of the university at which I taught. "Ohh," she said, her voice higher and the word drawn out. (She was more impressed.) The next cultural question: "What do you teach?" I answered, "I chair the Computer Information Systems department." This time she was very impressed. "Ohhhh," she said, her voice higher yet, and the word drawn out even further.

This incident reflects a modernist world view. In the modernist (techno-rational) viewpoint, theory ranks higher than practice; therefore, teaching at a university ranks higher than teaching at an elementary school. Also, science ranks higher than anything else; the closer one's occupation is to science, the higher it ranks. Therefore, teaching computers is ranked higher than teaching English. She would likely have been most impressed if I had been a physicist. The important thing here is that the dental assistant was totally unaware of the nature and source of her reactions; she was simply reacting from within the modernist paradigm. She was impressed according to the rules and didn't know it.

Also not long ago, I overheard a conversation between two young coeds. One said that she liked her English class better than her chemistry class. Why was that? asked the other. In chemistry, the first woman explained, there were right and wrong answers, but in English when "you, like, discuss a poem, it means, like, whatever you think it means." This was an example of the conflict of living in both the modern and postmodern worlds. When this young woman bemoaned the fact that chemistry had only right and wrong answers, she was reflecting a modernist paradigm; when she spoke of a poem meaning anything you want it to mean, she was espousing a radical postmodernist perspective on the absolute relativity of language isolated from the author's intentions or sociohistorical roots. Again, she was almost certainly unaware that she was reflecting elements of any paradigm.

The dueling-paradigm situation is also a major source of educational conflict in our society. David Elkind depicts elements of this conflict as it pertains to schools.[4] Although some of what he attributes to modernism and postmodernism may more accurately be considered cultural by-products emerging from these paradigms rather than being crucial to them, he offers his version of how the ideas of modernity and postmodernity have shaped our beliefs of how families and schools ought to look and act. According to Elkind, modernity gave us the idealized nuclear family depicted in the television shows *Ozzie and Harriet* and *Father Knows Best*. The ideal family had two parents (of different sexes) with a mother living a domestic home life and a father working at "the office"; family needs were more important than individual needs; child rearing was intuitive; children were innocent and needed protection; adolescents were immature and needed limitations and guidance from wise adults; social values were developed in the family from birth. The modern school reflects and reinforces the sentiments, values, and perceptions of this nuclear family. Therefore, the purpose of a school is to help children adjust to the larger society outside family boundaries and to maintain their innocence by sanitizing history, censoring literature, and ignoring cultural diversity. Emphasis is on teamwork and finding one's place in society. Both home and school are considered havens against a harsh world.

The nonidealized postmodern family frequently has either one parent or shared parenting with everyone working outside the home; individual needs take precedence over family interests; child rearing is learned; children are viewed as competent and adolescents as sophisticated. Elkind argues that single-parent and multiple-occupation families can no longer afford to view children as fragile because they *need* to have children who are more self-sufficient. These postmodern ideals are portrayed in the movie *Home Alone* (it wouldn't take a modern-paradigm family days to realize they had left a child behind) in which the child fends very well for himself and easily outwits bungling adults, and in the now-classic *Ferris Bueller's Day Off*, in which a sophisticated adolescent easily outwits an inept school principal and several sets of clueless adults. The postmodern school features full-day kindergartens for working parents, the gradual assumption of parental responsibilities, and more realistic curricula. Elkind also credits the postmodern school for the emphasis on individualistic self-esteem that prepares students for individual rather than group success.

Hybrid paradigms could easily be viewed as a source of creativity to spawn new ways of thinking. Yet, what makes this multiple-paradigm anxiety so problematic is that most people are unaware that we are living in a hybrid paradigm. Like King Louis, most of us go to bed nightly unaware that we are standing in a muck of shifting paradigms, but we are vaguely ill at ease, feeling as though the rules are constantly shifting, leaving us no place to stand. Because it is a paradigmatic change, we are not only faced with a conflict but an essentially invisible conflict. It is a schizophrenic experience, often requiring the coexistence of multiple paradigms. Walter Anderson beautifully illustrates this conflict:

> So, if you aspire to become president of the United States, you would do well to demonstrate that you are firmly rooted in the traditional American culture. Act like a white, middle-class family man and show up in church

once in a while. You don't want to be seen as too postmodern or too neo-
romantic: Do not say in public that you think truth is socially constructed.
If you meditate, keep it a secret. If you want to win an argument, let people know that your side is supported by scientific findings. Numbers are especially good. Even religious fundamentalists use science, whenever possible, to "prove" the truth of their beliefs; it is the lingua franca of public
discourse spoken (although in different accents) by all groups.[5]

Postmodernism is currently making deep inroads into our collective
world view. It is difficult to find a neat, concise definition for the term
*postmodernism*; because of its very essence, it is really a confluence of
viewpoints rather than one coherent school of thought. The paradigm is
often defined by what it isn't; what postmodernism isn't is modernism.
Modernism, sometimes termed enlightenment rationalism, logical positivism, and techno-rationalism, is the science-centered world view that replaced the religion-centered, autocratic world view of the Middle Ages.
As a thorough depiction of modernism and postmodernism could easily
overwhelm this book, I will limit this discussion to their contrasting views
of reality and science.

Modernism posits an unchangeable reality "out there" that can be discovered, described, and predicted through the use of science. Aligned with
this discovery of this fixed reality is the inevitable progress of humankind
through the use of scientific methods. Science provides the sole means by
which to discover and define this reality; any other practice is fanciful su-
perstition. The basic tenet of postmodernism is that the solitary, discover-
able, predictable, fixed reality of modernism does not exist. Instead of a
fixed truth explored through the use of science, we have multiple truths
existing only within our own relative contexts. Any universal truth is unknowable, as we cannot escape viewing it through some sort of cultural
lens. Science loses its status as the sole determiner of truth, since it is simply another cultural lens, another way of viewing the world.

But the fact that postmodernism is making inroads and that science is
no longer invincible does not mean modernism and science no longer play
important roles in our lives. Nor does the fact that modernism and science
still play an important part in our lives mean that the premodern ideas
have totally disappeared. As a result, we live our lives unaware of basic
paradigm conflict. The personal conflict resulting from living within these
warring paradigms is easily observable in the soft news section (often

named something like "Lifestyle" or "Variety") of every daily newspaper. In the same pages, one can normally find a horoscope, news concerning a new medical breakthrough, a diversity feature about the difficulty of a local immigrant group in maintaining its roots in this new culture, a Vatican news release concerning church doctrine on the ordination of women, one editorial extolling the need to make schools more accountable for student learning, another proclaiming the need for community progress in the form of a new strip mall being opposed by environmentalists, and a letter to the editor quoting biblical scripture as a basis for banning the teaching of evolution in public schools. The tension caused by this informational cacophony is understandable only by recognizing that each view represents a conflicting cultural paradigm. Anger and tension also build in opponents who become frustrated when their arguments are not persuasive to proponents of the opposing world views.

Although most individuals ignore these tensions by compartmentalizing their realities, some work to resolve the tensions and create new understandings by fusing them together to create a new, hybrid truth. For example, Donald Spoto, a popular biographer (and a theologian), wrote a book called *The Hidden Jesus*. This book demonstrates an adroit handling of multiple paradigms. In the introduction to this text, Spoto writes:

> There are many fine works of literary and historical criticism that will take you deeper into relevant matters of history, ancient culture, linguistic analysis and archeology, to name but a few of the fields that impact on contemporary biblical studies. . . . I hope to have brought to these reflections my years of training as a New Testament theologian and as a teacher of New Testament Studies.
>
> The Bible was, of course, written by human beings—it is the word of God in the words of men. Although those writers (and this author) affirm that they had been touched by transcendent realities, they were nevertheless bounded by the constraints of their own languages. All human discourse is metaphor—that is one of my major themes—and so any utterance about God must necessarily be provisional and incomplete, limited by the structures of language and the ideologies that constitute culture. For all that, I think that trying to speak of God is neither misguided effort nor lunacy.[6]

This clearly demonstrates the fusion of the three world views we have been considering. There are the premodern assertions that the Bible is the word of God (the sole, fixed reality) and that the truth of this reality was revealed to its writers. There are the modern assertions that foundational scientific analysis and professional preparation can help separate the transcendent wheat from the cultural chaff. Finally, this is all presented within a postmodern insistence that all human discourse concerning reality is limited by language and cultural baggage.

Each world view proclaims itself the only valid way of perceiving reality. Each emphasizes the flaws of competing paradigms and ignores its own flaws. In fact, each has important things to contribute, and each has flaws when its unique view is accepted as exclusive. There are no good and bad, right and wrong paradigms.

## Constructivism and Worldmaking

> Truth, far from being a solemn and severe master, is a docile and obedient servant.
>
>                              Nelson Goodman, *Ways of Worldmaking*
>                              (Indianapolis, Ind.: Hackett, 1978), 22.

A popular subset of the multifaceted postmodernism is *constructivism*. Constructivism says that although there may be an objective reality out there, it is impossible for us to see it because we view everything through cognitive lenses conditioned by the cultures in which we live. It is simply impossible to see reality directly, without cultural distortion. Constructivism refutes the modernist notion that human beings are empty vessels waiting to be filled with the truth if only they were all taught it correctly. Instead, all truth is internally constructed in interaction with our social environments. Truth is made, not found. One reason this is such a persuasive viewpoint is that much research has been done to demonstrate its validity. Another is that we have all had personal experiences that demonstrate it to ourselves.

For example, I recently went to see a movie in Chinese with English subtitles. I had always avoided subtitled movies in the past because I was certain I would not enjoy reading through a whole movie and having it detract from the visual experience. When I want to read, I sit home with a book. My recent experience challenges that viewpoint. I realized at the end of this enjoyable movie that I was only aware of the subtitles for the first few minutes of the movie. My mind quickly adjusted to them, and even though I continued to read lines, my mind transformed the words into internal dialogue as if I were listening to the actors speak them. Of course, they were speaking Chinese, and I was reading simple English translations of their words. I was both shocked and impressed by this cognitive trick. Friends to whom I proudly announced my amazing discovery were largely unimpressed with my cognitive cleverness because most of them have had similar experiences.

This, too can be viewed as a postmodern experience. First, there was the constructivist feat of reading written text and hearing it as if it were spoken word. Then, sitting just a bit beneath that was the fact that the movie was in Chinese and that intricate dialogues were being translated into short, readable English text. There was undoubtedly a richness to the movie that was denied to me as someone who does not speak Chinese. This emphasis on language is quintessentially postmodern. A solitary reality is not possible because we view the world through our languages, and languages cannot be totally translated. Essential aspects of world views are always lost in language translation.

I remember being touched by a poetry reading by Russian poet Yevgeny Yevtushenko. He would read a poem first in English, then in Russian. It was very clear that although his translated English poetry was very good, his native Russian poetry was stunning. Even without my understanding the language, the Russian tongue gave the poetry so much power and passion that was simply missing in English. Language is not neutral. It dictates the boundaries of our reality. It decides what will get our attention and what will not. Most people are aware that Eskimos have many different words for snow. This allows Eskimos to attribute distinctions to snow unavailable to other cultures. This is not just a matter of interpretation. Language literally provides them with a means to see snow differently than the rest of us, and thereby changes their relationship with it.

Foundational constructivist ideas were established in Berger and Luckmann's classic work, *The Social Construction of Reality*. They suggest that the sheer amount of sensory input available to us requires that we filter out most of it to maintain our sanity and to allow ourselves to function. Our reality is comprised of that portion of sensory input to which we give our attention. The act of bestowing our attention to sensory input is an act of reality construction. In addition to giving it attention, we attribute a myriad of cultural characteristics to it, and we view it as existing outside ourselves. Finally, after establishing an object as "out there" (separate from ourselves), it is our unique ability to then forget that we created the reality and the separation in the first place that makes us view our perception as reality. So after we create a ritual, a myth, or a belief, we forget we created it and assume it has always been so. The authors term this process *reification*. "Reification implies that man is capable of forgetting his own authorship of the human world, and further that the dialectic between man, the producer, and his products is lost to consciousness."[7] What we call reality, then, is a description provided by society that becomes the correct way of looking at the world. This creates a basic dialectic in which a social paradigm exists only through individual acceptance of the description provided by that paradigm.

As our understanding of the universe is completely bounded by the limitations of our senses, I find a radio station analogy helpful for understanding the concept of constructivism. We are surrounded by radio waves from a multitude of radio stations; this corresponds to the vast number of sensory inputs available to us at any instant. We do not deal with these radio waves directly. We use a radio tuner to select a station from the multitude of stations existing "out there"; if we could not do this, the resulting cacophony of sounds would be unintelligible and maddening. We use our attention to filter through the sensory inputs and select those with which we wish to deal. We choose a radio station on the basis of our age, geographic location, education, socioeconomic group, etc. Some people like classical music, some jazz, and others country-western. We filter our real-life sensory inputs largely on the basis of these same items. Finally, there are radio stations outside of our range; there are those we prefer, avoid, reject. Even those we prefer might be distorted by static or be unavailable. All the same holds true in our socially constructed reality.

A vital concept that has influenced my journey is the idea of *worldmaking*. This is a constructivist idea that emerged from Nelson Goodman's classic work, *Ways of Worldmaking*. Goodman acknowledges in his introduction that his book would bring a whole new mainstream dimension to philosophy.

> I think of this book as belonging in that mainstream of modern philosophy that began when Kant exchanged the structure of the world for the structure of the mind, continued when C. I. Lewis exchanged the structure of the mind for the structure of concepts, and that now proceeds to exchange the struc-

ture of the several symbol systems of the sciences, philosophy, the arts, perception, and everyday discourse. The movement is from unique truth and a world fixed and found to a diversity of right and even conflicting versions or worlds in the making.[8]

Goodman argues, as did Berger and Luckmann, that the truth is simply beyond human comprehension because *truth* is too huge and too changeable for us to grasp. The small pieces of truth we can grasp are distortions we cannot trust. The truth we discover is more a matter of finding a fit than it is finding a universal fact. Goodman says that what we take for reality is mostly a matter of habit in the same way that we attribute reality to a movie or a painting when in fact they are both creative representations of reality. "Discovering laws involves drafting them. Recognizing patterns is very much a matter of inventing and imposing them. Comprehension and creation go on together."[9] According to Goodman, we tend to find that for which we are looking, reversing the old adage that seeing is believing.

*Reminder to readers:* One of the most difficult things trainers face with athletes new to weight training is getting them to increase weight and repetitions gradually. The same rules apply here. Remember to increase your theory gradually. If you are a veteran theorist, please dive into the next section on postmodern science. If you are new to theory, feel free to skip the next section and jump to the concluding section of this chapter, "The Place on Which We Stand." Remember, you can always return to it later.

## POSTMODERN SCIENCE

It isn't just that Bohr's atom with its electron "orbits" is a false picture; all pictures are false, and there is no physical analogy we can make to understand what goes on inside atoms. Atoms behave like atoms, nothing else.

John Gribbin, *In Search of Schrödinger's Cat: Quantum Physics and Reality* (New York: Bantam, 1984), 92.

The modern age began to systematically replace the medieval paradigm once science provided a description of reality that exposed the inherent weaknesses in the theocratic view. Similarly, postmodernism gained a foothold when the central scientific tenets of modernism began to show cracks. Large strides toward this end were accomplished with the publication of Thomas Kuhn's *The Structure of Scientific Revolutions*, which demonstrated that science, too, is restricted by the paradigms within which it operates. Ironically, classical science was called into question by the scientific community itself with the development of quantum theory and the theories of relativity.

Kuhn has been influential is causing a reexamination of what we call science. Kuhn explains that time and place play a role in the "beliefs" of a scientific community. Like Goodman, he views reality as something that is malleable but not an altogether arbitrary construction.

> According to Kuhn, reality, as it is generally referred to in everyday scientific contexts, is a phenomenal world, not the (only possible) phenomenal world, and certainly not the world-in-itself. . . . But it's by no means a whimsical construction, an arbitrary invention of consciousness.[10]

Kuhn presents a historical view of science to demonstrate the power of paradigms in the practice of science. He describes a Hanover Institute experiment in which individuals provided with identical retinal impressions see different things and another in which individuals provided with different retinal impressions see the same thing. The latter was an experiment using glasses that flipped the visual world of the wearer upside down. After a period of disorientation (similar to my experience with movie subtitles), the wearers cognitively flipped the world right side up and were able to conduct business as usual. Kuhn explores how the "discovery" of Neptune was delayed despite the existence of adequate technical equipment accompanied by the routine scanning of the skies. Although this celestial body had been observed repeatedly for nearly a century, it was not identified as a planet until it no longer fit existing perceptual categories.

These revolutionary insights involve more than mere scientific reinterpretation; Kuhn emphasizes that they involve redefinitions of the actual reality in which we live.

> Surveying the rich experimental literature from which these examples are drawn makes one suspect that something like a paradigm is prerequisite to perception itself. What a man sees depends both upon what he looks at and also upon what his previous visual–conceptual experience has taught him to see.[11]

Such redefinitions take place only in periods of crisis when what we know fails to fit prevailing paradigms. Kuhn identified the period in physics when light sometimes seemed to be a wave and sometimes seemed to be a particle as such a period of crisis, leading to the development of wave mechanics and the realization that light was different than either a wave or a particle.[12] It was this crisis from within the scientific community itself that accentuated the cracks in the classical scientific (and modernist) world view. It is not accidental that the rise of postmodernism in the early twentieth century has been concurrent with the emergence of quantum theory and Einstein's theories of relativity.

## Relativity and Quantum Mechanics

Anyone who is not shocked by quantum theory has not understood it.

John Gribbin, *In Search of Schrödinger's Cat: Quantum Physics and Reality* (New York: Bantam, 1984), 5.

Quantum theory was born at the turn of the twentieth century in response to the scientific crisis alluded to by Kuhn. The crisis developed at a time when the prevailing theory used to describe the behavior of light was Wave Theory, which depicted light in terms of continuous waves. The crisis began when Max Planck showed that light could be measured as individual "quanta" as well as continuous waves. From this, Einstein developed his theory of Photoelectric Effect, which determined that light is made up of individual packets of energy, with the color of each packet indicating its energy level. Quantum theory was born from the crisis that resulted when classical theory stated that light *must* be made up of waves, and Einstein stated that light *must* be made up of packets of energy. In fact, light sometimes acts like waves and sometimes acts like packets, and neither theory is able to explain both behaviors. The paradox is that both theories seem to be true even though our understanding of light doesn't have a "wave + packet" explanation. Quantum mechanics was further developed by Niels Bohr's depiction of atomic structure, de Broglie's mathematical proposition that particles exhibit wavelike properties, and Schrödinger's work on the probability of finding a particular particle in a particular point in space.

Heisenberg's Uncertainty Principle states that the more we know about a particle's position, the less we know about its velocity (and direction),

and the more we know about a particle's velocity, the less we know about
its position. Schrödinger's wave function approach describes the statistical probability of finding a particular particle in any given place at any
given time. These two theories highlight the difficulties of quantum
physics, as the act of observing an event at the subatomic level changes it.
There is no such thing as objective observation, since the very act of observation influences the outcome to an undetermined extent. This flies in
the face of the classical scientific approach of "observe, theorize, experiment, and validate," since the observe and experiment phases are not re-
peatable. Heisenberg's and Schrödinger's theories basically say that the
universe is not predictable because we can't reliably observe it, and we
can never have enough information about it to make predictions because
the more we know about some aspects of it, the less we know about other
aspects.

The cornerstones of classical science, causality and determinism, are
thereby dealt a death blow. According to the classical macroscopic world
of Newtonian physics, if one billiard ball of a given velocity and direction
hits another, it is always possible to accurately predict the velocity and direction of the ball it hits, since the amount of energy introduced to the experiment is negligble. At the subatomic level where the magnitude of energy introduced is significant, the result of a particle collision can only be
predicted in terms of probabilities. Thus, quantum theory destroyed the
classical assumption that a system's physical state could be precisely measured and that its future states could be predicted.

> In the evolution of quantum physics the barrier between man, peering dimly
> through the clouded windows of his senses, and whatever objective reality
> may exist has been rendered almost impassable. For whenever he attempts
> to penetrate and spy on the "real" objective world, he changes and distorts
> its workings by the very process of his observation. And when he tries to di-
> vorce this "real" world from his sense perceptions he is left with nothing but
> a mathematical scheme. He is indeed somewhat in the position of a blind
> man trying to discern the shape and texture of a snowflake. As soon as it
> touches his fingers or his tongue it dissolves. [13]

Einstein's theories of special and general relativity equally rocked the
foundations of the modern world. His laws of relativity "provide a com-

prehensive picture of an incredibly complex universe in which the simple mechanical events of our earthly experience are the exceptions."[14] His Special Theory of Relativity states that all observations are only valid for their particular inertial frames of reference. It also states that the speed of light is an absolute frame of reference, as it is the absolute constant between all frames of reference. This law fundamentally changes the way we view the commonsense world of our senses. As physical laws are valid only in similar systems, changing the speed of that system (in relation to the speed of light) causes matter to change, causing measuring rods to lengthen or shorten and clocks to run faster or slower. And we do not notice the changes if we are within that system; the change is apparent only when compared to other systems. There is no such thing as absolute time or absolute speed.

Because there is no way to judge absolutes, time and space are absolutes only within our limited sensory worlds. It is for this reason that we are reluctant as humans to accept that time and space are simply forms of human perception. Einstein proves that space-time is not the same between different inertial frames of reference; all time is measured in terms of its relationship to physical phenomena such as the rotation of the Earth and the movement of the Earth around the sun. Likewise space has meaning only in its relationship to time. Space is measured in terms of the time and velocity it takes for an object to move between masses. Thus, physicists, rather than using the terms *time* or *space*, now speak in terms of a *space-time* continuum. Everything in the universe is relative. Certainty exists only within our limited sensory perceptions because we all share a world moving at a similar speed.

So although in premodern times we "knew" that the sun revolved around the Earth, and in modern times we "knew" that the Earth revolved around the sun at a rate of twenty-two miles per second, we now "know" that, in reality, everything is moving in relation to everything else. Special Relativity says that we don't experientially recognize any of this movement because we are part of the same rotational system.

Contrary to popular belief the moon does not revolve around the earth; they revolve around each other—or, more precisely, around a common center of gravity. The entire solar system, moreover, is moving within the local star system at a rate of 13 miles a second; the local star system is moving with

the Milky Way at the rate of 200 miles a second, and the whole Milky Way
is drifting with respect to the remote external galaxies at the rate of 100
miles a second—and all in different directions.[15]

Special Relativity also accounts for mass-energy equivalence (almost
everyone is familiar with $E=mc^2$). Prior to Einstein, mass and energy were
considered to be separate substances. Einstein demonstrated that mass is
simply concentrated energy and that the universe is a dance of shifting energy and mass. Space is filled with subatomic particles such as *muons*
(subatomic particles that exist for less than a millionth of a second), flash-
ing briefly in and out of existence.

Einstein's Special Relativity established this equivalence of mass and
energy, and his Theory of General Relativity established the indivisibility
of the space-time continuum with his description of gravity as the effect of
curved space-time. "Prior to Einstein the universe was most commonly
pictured as an island of matter afloat in the center of an infinite sea of
space."[16] General Relativity eradicates the notion of a rigid, barren space
holding orbiting matter in place by a vague gravitational pull and replaces
it with a live, changing continuum of matter and motion. "Just as a fish
swimming in the sea agitates the water around it, so a star, a comet, or a
galaxy distorts the geometry of the space-time through which it moves."[17]
This effectively changes the isolated, impersonal universe in which we live
into a world of interconnecting, interacting forms of connected energy.

Even with this brief overview (see figure 2.2) of the "new science," it
becomes quickly apparent that quantum theory and relativity create and
support the relativistic tenets of postmodernism.

Man's inescapable impasse is that he himself is part of the world he seeks
to explore; his body and proud brain are mosaics of the same elemental particles that compose the dark, drifting clouds of interstellar space; he is, in
the final analysis, merely an ephemeral conformation of the primordial
space-time field. Standing midway between macrocosm and microcosm he
finds barriers on every side and can perhaps but marvel, as St. Paul did nine-
teen hundred years ago, that "the world was created by the word of God so
that what is seen was made out of things which do not appear."[18]

Most of the quantum scientists were disturbed by their anti-intuitive findings. "For what quantum mechanics says is that nothing is real and that we

cannot say anything about the things we are doing when we are not looking at them."[19] Schrödinger said he didn't like the results of his work and was sorry he ever had anything to do with it.[20] Einstein was greatly troubled by the essentially postmodern truth displayed by his theories, which he felt represented quirky mathematical tricks that just happened to describe atomic and subatomic behavior. For the rest of his life, Einstein sought a "unified field theory" that would closely correspond to our everyday sense of reality and that would remove the randomness from the universe created by his theories. He is well known for having said, "God doesn't play dice with the universe." He died without successfully developing his unified theory. But other attempts at a single one-explains-all theory continue (see figure 2.2).

In the midst of this pursuit of randomness and relativity, the ground continues to shift, and mathematical physics is moving further away from classical science. Capra, in his *Tao of Physics*,[21] quotes Robert Oppenheimer, Niels Bohr, and Werner Heisenberg describing parallels between quantum physics and Eastern mysticism. Theorists such as d'Epagnat and

| Classical | Quantum |
|---|---|
| **Causality/Determinism:** everything is caused by that which came before it; laws accurately predict with the results of prior actions | **Uncertainty:** future and past are malleable and indeterminate; mathematics states results as probabilities |
| **Possibility:** things are possible or impossible; mechanical explanation | **Probability:** anything is possible but is predictable only as probability; mathematical explanation |
| **Replicable Results:** identical experiments yield identical, predicable results | **Aggregate Results:** similar results are possible only in aggregate; probability determines the individual results |
| **Objective Observation:** objective observation is possible because observer is outside of experiment | **Participant Observation:** objective observation is impossible because observer influences experiment |
| **Static Reality:** reality is objective and unchanging | **Changing Reality:** reality is always changing |
| **Objective Clocklike Reality:** reality separate from observer (described in terms of mechanical laws); reality operates predictably like a machine; our choices, bound by machine-like determinism, are limited | **Malleable Random Reality:** reality interactive with observer (described in terms of mathematics) changes constantly, and objective observations are not possible; we are connected to nature and gain freedom of choice |

**Figure 2.2   Classical and Quantum Viewpoints**

Bohm argue that everything is literally connected to everything else as interacting particles that came into being together at the beginning of the universe.[22] This theory maintains that "every particle in every star and galaxy that we can see 'knows' about the existence of every other particle."[23] Other physicists like Oxford's David Deutsch believe that quantum theory

will be a pathway, a component of some future, more unifying theory which will involve among other things the General Theory of Relativity. But also I think it will involve areas which are now not even considered part of physics.[24]

There are other serious scientific developments that strain our credibility and creep across the line into science fiction, virtually *theoretical theory*: "there are developments in store as far beyond those that quantum mechanics has already given us as those developments are beyond classical devices."[25]

at the quantum level particles seem to be involved in time travel all the "time," and Frank Tipler has shown that the equations of general relativity permit time travel. It is possible to conceive of a kind of genuine travel forward and backward in time that does not permit paradoxes, and such a form of time travel depends on the reality of different universes.[26]

This includes such ideas as quantum computers, multiple parallel realities, and quantum foam. Quantum computers may be thousands or millions of times faster than today's digital computers, which are limited by banks of on/off digital switches. Quantum computers, instead, are assembled from molecular units knows as qubits. Qubits, unlike digital switches that can exist only in two different states, are capable of simultaneously being in an endless number of states.

Researchers say that while a classical computer bit can be either black or white, a qubit could simultaneously take on all the colors of the spectrum. Thus a quantum computer could do many calculations simultaneously.[27]

Quantum technology is expected to become a viable option by the second decade of this century, when transistor-based digital chips are expected to reach a physical efficiency limit. Currently, the most powerful quantum computers operate on three or four qubits; it is expected that several hundred qubits will be necessary to perform any useful computation.[28] The possibility of being able to harness multiple-state particles would provide an extraordinary increase in computing power.

Another idea emerging from quantum mechanics is the concept of multiple parallel universes. This concept is often captured in the word *multiverse,* which contrasts sharply with our traditional use of the word *universe.* This concept emerges as an explanation for the interference effects of single-photon-at-a-time experiments, positing weak interference effects from parallel universes. Gribbin offered this as a solution to Schrödinger's thought problem about placing a theoretical cat in a box with radiation that will eventually kill the cat, and asking whether the cat would be alive or dead at any given time an observer opens the box. The famous Copenhagen Interpretation states that the cat is neither dead nor alive until an observer opens the box and finds it in one state or another. At that point, the observer's act of observation collapses the probabilities into reality.

Hugh Everett's "many worlds" (multiverse) interpretation, though resting on sound mathematical ground, has been resisted by the physics community because it implies the existence of an infinite number of worlds parallel to but separate from our own universe. This is an idea that runs counter to our intuitive understanding of the world and naturally makes us uneasy. For Everett, the act of observing Schrödinger's cat creates two different realities, one in which the observer finds a live cat and another in which the observer finds a dead cat. And utilizing Einstein's Special Relativity, the observer in either case would be unaware of the split because each is a separate self-contained, self-referential system; Everett says this is no different than that fact that we don't feel the orbital motion of the Earth around the sun. Physicists Deutsch and Lockwood argue in *Scientific American* that if the multiverse exists, space-time travel is possible.[29] Everett explains further:

What happens when we make a measurement at the quantum level is that we are forced by the process of observation to select one of these alternatives, which becomes part of what we see as the "real" world; the act of observation cuts the ties that bind alternative realities together, and allows them to go on their own separate ways through superspace, each alternative reality containing its own observer who has made the same observation but got a different quantum "answer" and thinks that he has "collapsed the wave function" into one single quantum alternative.[30]

Finally, the study of quantum gravity predicts that the structure of space-time is not the gentle curves predicted by general relativity. This results in the concept of quantum foam, an irregular, subatomic, space-time remnant of the Big Bang birth of the universe described as a fuzzy or foamy structure. Some theorists suggest that it may contain wormholes that would facilitate space-time travel. "At the quantum level, space-time itself may be very complex topologically, with 'wormholes' and 'bridges' connecting different regions of space-time."[31] Some theory suggests that quantum foam might serve as a gateway to the alternate worlds described by Everett. "A spaceship that size could find itself negotiating virtual black holes, or getting sucked into one wormhole after another and tossed back and forth in time and space."[32]

## THE PLACE ON WHICH WE STAND

Nothing is real unless it is observed.

John Gribbin, *In Search of Schrödinger's Cat: Quantum Physics and Reality* (New York: Bantam Books), 3.

So where are we able to stand? We live terrified that if we think about and embrace the ideas of postmodernism and quantum mechanics, we will have nowhere left to stand, no point of stability from which to live our lives. In returning to our search for answers about teaching and learning, it is time to ask what ideas presented so far are at all helpful to us; it is time to find a place to stand in what appears to be a sea of relativity, a sea of quantum foam.

Although the relativity of postmodernism frightens most people and angers some, it emerges from problems within the modernist world view. And although the relativity of quantum mechanics filled even its own creators with feelings of deficiency and regret, it emerged from problems within the field of traditional science. It seems that the main points of postmodernism and quantum mechanics are simply irrefutable. To ignore either is to live in the past. It seems to me that the discomfort we feel living in the quantum foam is alleviated with one simple idea: we are not done yet.

We tend to view our historical development through time as ending with our time. We feel that we did evolve and develop as living beings and now we are done—how we look, and how we think, act, and view the world will remain static for the rest of time. This, of course, is ludicrous. Our way of looking at reality will (and must) continue to evolve. Holes in postmodernism are already apparent, and new world views will incorporate and replace it in the same way it incorporated and replaced modernism.

There is a reason why I chose to discuss both postmodernism and quantum physics in this chapter. Although postmodernism is more directly applicable to our questions about teaching, quantum physics has a head start on the philosophy and hints at the direction postmodernism may be heading. As modern physics sounds increasingly like Eastern mysticism, quantum scientists continue to explore the modern equivalent of Einstein's Unified Field Theory. Physicists like David Deutsch seem to feel that a more unifying theory is inevitable. It seems even more inevitable that postmodernism will evolve into a philosophical unified field theory. Some aspects of postmodernism will survive and some will not. More importantly, we will continue to explore reality and come to terms with the fact that we are limited beings, incapable of experiencing the totality of raw reality, incapable of knowing everything through our limited powers of cognition and reason, incapable of standing separate from everything else.

Some current postmodern ideas that seem to be on safe ground are useful to our exploration. One is the moderate postmodern idea of constructivism. This concept enthralled me from the first time I encountered it. Again, it says that although an incomprehensible reality may exist "out there," we deal only with infinitesimal portions of it. The universe is essentially unknowable because we are constrained by both biological and cultural limitations. Our senses are very limiting, and the "common-sense" reality we create becomes the touchstone against which all ideas are judged.

as Einstein pointed out, common sense is actually nothing more than a deposit of prejudices laid down in the mind prior to the age of eighteen. Every

new idea one encounters in later years must combat this accretion of "self-
evident" concepts.[33]

We live within a mysterious and inexplicable sliver of distorted reality
that we mistake for a totality. Any reality is simply beyond our limited
grasp. Our rational brains are no more built to understand raw, unfiltered
reality than a goldfish brain is capable of understanding a microprocessor
chip.

We are like the mythical blind men describing the elephant. Due to their
blindness, none of them are aware that they are describing only an ap-
pendage. Reading this parable, we smirk, knowing the blind men are describing only a part of the elephant, ascribing to it characteristics of what
they already know. That smirk quickly fades, however, when we come to
understand that we are not so different. When we describe reality from a
modernist perspective, like the blind men, we describe only a sliver of reality, and we share their unawareness that something greater lies just beyond it. Postmodernism's vital contribution is to make us aware that it is
only a distorted sliver of a greater elephant that we may never be able to
fully grasp. We are simply worldmaking entities who have no choice but
to live in our worlds of trunks and tails and legs.

As worldmakers, we are active participants in the creation of the realities in which we live. Our situation within a particular time and place affects our reality construction. We create reality, first by choosing the portions of reality with which we intend to deal, and second by overlaying
our experiential and cultural expectations on that portion of reality. We
then objectify our choices as "reality" by ignoring the fact that we have
made the choices.

Researchers have found that, at least at the micro level, cause and effect determinism is limited and that the act of observation affects the outcome of what is being studied. Qualitative researchers have demonstrated
the observer effect in conducting macro world research as well. The observer is part of nature, part of the problem, part of the solution; the act of
research influences the problem and the solution. "Objective" modernist
research is meaningful only for problems within a certain range of study,
and modernism diminishes the validity and importance of problems outside this range. Even when we know that something works, we often don't
know *how* it works or *why* it works. Einstein found that his mathematics

accurately described the subatomic universe, and he was actually disappointed that it did.

We know that other forces are at work and that many forces are interconnected. Our individual acts are awash in a sea of other relational influences. Just as the view of solitary planets moving in lonely orbits in solitary space has given way to a view of planets swimming through space leaving fishlike wakes, so our individual acts are part of a collective act, connecting with history and culture, interactive with other people and objects. Just as the view of isolated electrons orbiting dense electrons has given way to one of particles that still recognize each other from the Big Bang, we begin to realize our very real connection to each other.

Now that we have a clearer picture of where we stand in the quantum foam, it is important to find out where we stand in relation to education and to teaching.

## NOTES

1. Donald A. Schön, *The Reflective Practitioner: How Professionals Think in Action* (San Francisco, Calif.: Basic Books, 1983), 165.

2. Lee Canter and Marlene Canter, *Assertive Discipline: Positive Behavior Management for Today's Classroom* (Santa Monica, Calif.: Lee Canter and Associates, 1992), 9.

3. Lee Canter, "Let the Educator Beware: A Response to Curwin and Mendler," *Educational Leadership* 46, no 2 (October 1988): 73.

4. David Elkind, "School and Family in the Postmodern World," *Phi Delta Kappan* 77, no 1 (September 1995): 8–14.

5. Walter Truett Anderson, "Four Different Ways to Be Absolutely Right," in *The Truth about the Truth*, ed. Walter Truett Anderson (New York: Tarcher Putnam, 1995), 113–114.

6. Donald Spoto, *The Hidden Jesus: A New Life* (New York: St. Martin's Press, 1998), xvi–xviii.

7. Peter L. Berger and Thomas Luckmann, *The Social Construction of Reality: A Treatise in the Sociology of Knowledge* (1966; reprint, New York: Anchor Books, 1989), 89.

8. Nelson Goodman, *Ways of Worldmaking* (Indianapolis, Ind.: Hackett, 1987), x.

9. Goodman, *Worldmaking*, 22.

10. Paul Hoyningen-Huene, *Reconstructing Scientific Revolutions: Thomas S. Kuhn's Philosophy of Science* (Chicago: University of Chicago Press, 1993), 267.

11. Thomas S. Kuhn, *The Structure of Scientific Revolutions,* 2d ed. (Chicago: University of Chicago Press, 1970), 113.

12. Kuhn, *Revolutions,* 114.

13. Lincoln Barnett, *The Universe and Dr. Einstein* (New York: Bantam, 1978), 35.

14. Barnett, *Dr. Einstein,* 59.

15. Barnett, *Dr. Einstein,* 39–40.

16. Barnett, *Dr. Einstein,* 93.

17. Barnett, *Dr. Einstein,* 85.

18. Barnett, *Dr. Einstein,* 117–118.

19. John Gribbin, *In Search of Schrödinger's Cat: Quantum Physics and Reality* (New York: Bantam, 1984), 2.

20. Gribbin, *Schrödinger's Cat,* v.

21. Fritjof Capra, *The Tao of Physics: An Exploration of the Parallels between Modern Physics and Eastern Mysticism* (1975; reprint, Boston: Shambala, 1985), 18.

22. Gribbin, *Schrödinger's Cat,* 229–230.

23. Gribbin, *Schrödinger's Cat,* 231.

24. Filiz Peach, "David Deutsch interviewed by Filiz Peach," *Philosophy Now* 30 (December/January 2000), 24.

25. Gribbin, *Schrödinger's Cat,* 233.

26. Gribbin, *Schrödinger's Cat,* 248.

27. John Markoff, "Quantum Computing Is Becoming More than Just a Good Idea," *New York Times on the Web,* www.nytimes.com (April 28, 1998): 2.

28. Peach, "Deutsch," 27.

29. David Deutsch and Michael Lockwood, "The Quantum Physics of Time Travel," *Scientific American* 270, no. 3 (March 1994).

30. Quoted in Gribbin, *Schrödinger's Cat,* 237.

31. Gribbin, *Schrödinger's Cat,* 261.

32. Michael Lewes Brookes, "Quantum Foam," *New Scientist* 28, no 2191 (19 June 1999): 2.

33. Barnett, *Dr. Einstein,* 58.

*Chapter Three*

# The Paradox of Teaching and Learning

The paradox of learning a really new competence is this: that a student cannot at first understand what he needs to learn, can learn it only by educating himself, and can educate himself only by beginning to do what he does not yet understand.

> Donald A. Schön, *Educating the Reflective Practitioner: Toward a New Design in Teaching and Learning in the Professions* (San Francisco, Calif.: Jossey-Bass, 1987), 93.

## TRANSFORMATIONS OF VISION

In his *Structure of Scientific Revolutions*, Kuhn makes a point that becomes vitally important as we turn our attention from foundational ideas back to questions of education. He described broken lines on a bubble-chamber photograph as being confusing to a physics student even though they are familiar to a physicist. He indicates that in order for the student to see and respond to this photograph as the scientist does, the student will need to undergo a number of "transformations of vision" because the student is not entering a fixed world. "Rather, it is determined jointly by the environment and the particular normal-science tradition that the student has been trained to pursue."[1] For Kuhn, then, a major part of education involves initiation into the cultural vision of a new paradigm, an initiation that begins the process of creating its truth.

So facts are not really independent of the observer and his theories and preconceptions. However, at any one time, in any one culture, it is usually possible for most observers to agree on them. To put it better, facts are what all observers agree on.[2]

A student striving to become a scientist or a teacher or a poet needs to undergo such a transformation of vision to gain access to the agreed-upon facts of that world. This recognition of the need for world view transformation brings us to the important work of Donald Schön, whose critique of techno-rationalism was introduced in the previous chapter.

## DONALD SCHÖN AND PROFESSIONAL EDUCATION

Schön is well known for his study of reflective practice in professional education. His work is a fundamental cornerstone for answers to the questions I asked myself when I began my research. Although he emphasizes the education of professionals, the key ideas of his work easily cut across all education, at all levels, in both the professions and the liberal arts. His views explain much about my own experience in becoming a "computer person." Yet, I found that the world view transformation of which he speaks is equally applicable to my study of English as to my study of computers.

When I coached basketball, I needed to take courses to obtain a coaching certificate. One of the courses that I needed to take was taught by an assistant football coach who was incapable of thinking or talking outside of a football context. As this was immediately apparent, I simply began to translate his football-speak into a context that would help me coach basketball (not unlike my "translation" of the subtitles in the movie I mentioned in chapter 1). So at this juncture, I ask the reader to keep in mind that the word *professional*, although a natural derivative of Schön's work, rightfully includes all education. Feel free to translate my *professional* viewpoint into one that better fits you and your situation.

Schön's study starts with a critique of the modernist/scientific paradigm (which he calls positivism or techno-rationalism) and its prescription for professional education. Because science is the backbone of positivism, he argues, professions need to be steeped in theory and science in order to establish legitimacy. For this reason, professions tend to emphasize theory and research and to minimize practical application, which is generally attached toward the end of a program following the "real" study. Although this tradition has given professions legitimacy, he continues, it has also preordained that professions will only be able to deal effectively with largely irrelevant theoretical problems while ignoring more relevant problems of application.

Schön adapts the worldmaking perspectives of Goodman to form a constructivist view of professional practice. He argues against the limitations of the positivist perspective, which values theory above practice and orders itself with basic science at the top, applied science in the middle, and practical technical skills at the bottom. We can see this hierarchy at a glance in postsecondary education with its large, prestigious research universities at the top, professional practice universities with a liberal arts base in the middle, and technical/vocational colleges with minimal liberal arts at the bottom. This hierarchy is also apparent in the work world, where the people farthest removed from the actual work of any organization have the highest salaries, prestige, and power while the people who actually do the work eke out meager wages and have little, if any, prestige or power. Making an analogy of a "high plateau" and a "low swamp,"[3] Schön maintains that positivism deals with the clearly delineated but less important problems perched at the top of the plateau but fails miserably with the messy professional-practice problems in the swamp below, which require practitioners to deal effectively with uncertainty.

> The dean of a well-known school of management [William Pownes] observed a decade ago that "we need most to teach students how to make decisions under conditions of uncertainty, but this is just what we don't know how to teach."[4]

Schön counters popular mythology by arguing that outstanding practitioners do not have more professional knowledge; rather, they have more wisdom, talent, intuition, or artistry.[5] It is understandable that most politically inspired teacher education reforms have run counter to this insight and have stressed the need for more knowledge. It is easier to require more knowledge, as knowledge is thought to be objective and measurable. It is more difficult to imagine a national call for more wisdom and intuition. Such a call would evoke considerable sniggering and would be more difficult to define, measure, and demonstrate. The modernist perspective also assumes that because wisdom and intuition are too subtle and complex for measurement, they clearly cannot to be learned or taught. This dilemma demonstrates Schön's lament about "low swamp" problems. Down in the swamp, we know what is necessary to solve the problem, but we are denied this solution simply because it is too difficult to envision and too messy to implement.

Yet intuition *is* observable and *is* learnable. I remember being a young high school teacher standing outside the cafeteria doors during lunch supervision. I was talking with the dean of students, a wily veteran of some thirty years, when a student walked up to the soft drink machine near the doors. The young man dropped his coins into the slot, pressed the button for his selection, and got . . . nothing. He pressed the button again. Nothing. He pounded on the button for his selection. Then he kicked the machine.

As a young teacher, I was curious to see how a veteran dean of students would handle this situation. In the high school I attended, he would have grabbed the student by the neck, hauled him forcefully to the office, thrown him into a chair, conducted a lecture about respect for school property, and assigned some sort of atonement to make the student reluctant to repeat his actions. This dean, however, was different. He looked at the student and laughed. "Don't you know you have to put money in the machine to get something?" he asked, knowing well that the student had put money in it and that the student knew he knew. When he said this, the student laughed too. The dean quietly told him to fill out a form in the office to get his money back.

This was an observable act of wisdom, talent, intuition, and artistry. While it wouldn't work everywhere or with everyone, it was brilliant in this case. The problem was a student kicking the machine. This dean understood that he needed to get the student to stop kicking the machine, not to secure dominance over or to seek retribution from him. With the proper attitude and with one sentence, the dean got the student to stop kicking the machine, to laugh, and to walk away with dignity.

I have found such wisdom/intuition to be indirectly learnable and teachable. This single observation deeply influenced my own world view of effective student interactions. Two incidents demonstrating this influence leap immediately to mind. The first took place in a tenth grade study hall of about forty students. The study hall was in a large traditional classroom with a teacher desk in front and rows of student desks facing it. As I sat at my desk reading, the students were in front of me, with the doorway and a trash can to my immediate left. In the distant right corner of the room sat Kevin; in the distant left corner sat Katie. I was rereading a novel I would be using soon in my English class, monitoring the class out of my peripheral vision. Suddenly, Kevin got out of his seat, sauntered up the rightmost aisle, and crossed in front of my desk, heading for the wastebasket. When he arrived, he noisily crumpled up a sheet of paper and plopped it into the basket. He flashed the class a satisfied look and sauntered back to his seat. I neither looked up nor said anything. A few minutes later, Kevin got up again, sauntered past my desk a second time, and made a bigger show of crumpling the paper and tossing it in the basket before returning to his seat. It was a superb performance, but I neither looked up nor said anything.

By this time, Katie could barely contain herself. Scant seconds after Kevin returned to his seat the second time, Katie popped up and took her turn sauntering and crumpling. By this time, I could feel the other thirty-eight pairs of eyes on me, watching to see what I was going to do. I feigned reading and said nothing. Katie's backside had scarcely hit her seat, when Kevin jumped up to make his third trip. As he passed in front of my desk, I said one sentence that ended everything. Without looking up, I said, "You're going to have to stop meeting like this." The study hall erupted in a roar of laughter. Kevin and Katie turned red. And then— everyone got back to work. This was intuition at work; the words had formed suddenly in my mind as Kevin passed in front of my desk the third time, and I simply knew it would work. It followed the dean's example. The problem ended. Dignity was intact. And I never did look up.

The second example was a time when I broke up a fight in the school commons. I saw two seniors fighting, with the inevitable bloodthirsty crowd circled around them. It was obvious that Eddie (an advisee of mine) held a big advantage over the other student and was going to hurt him. Although I hated wading into fights, I pushed through the crowd, touched Eddie on the shoulder, and said quietly near his ear, "Eddie, that's enough." It was totally instinctive, as I had had no idea what I was going to do as I had waded through the onlookers. Eddie immediately stopped fighting and ran off down the hall. The fight ended, the crowd broke up, and the other student was happy to not be destroyed by Eddie.

I returned to my classroom. A short time later, Eddie showed up at my door. Awkwardly shifting his weight from one foot to the other, he asked, "So what did you say to me out there?" I told him. He said, "I knew you said something, but I didn't know what it was." Eddie stared at the floor. "Thanks," he said. Other students later explained to me that the student Eddie had been annihilating had sold drugs to Eddie's younger brother. This had enraged Eddie, who had decided to make sure it wouldn't happen again, and he had gotten a little carried away. This again illustrates the importance of Schön's contention that it isn't more knowledge that is necessary; what is necessary is knowing how to read a situation and make creative use of what we do know. Wading into a fight can be a dangerous thing. Touching someone who is enraged on the shoulder and saying something quietly to him could get you hurt. Yet in this case, it was exactly the correct action, and I knew it.

I can only imagine someone trying to turn such intuition into knowledge by creating a series of five steps for breaking up a fight:

A Fantasy: Steps for Breaking up Fights (use as many of the steps as necessary)

1. Disperse the audience: Loudly announce to students gathered around the fight that they are all to return to their classes immediately.
2. Establish a consequence: Once students have dispersed, loudly announce to the combatants that they should cease their fighting immediately and that both will be receiving a check after their names.
3. Increase the consequence: If they do not cease their fighting, loudly announce that they will each receive an addition check after their names and will receive a detention at the end of the day.
4. Establish the maximum consequence: If they do not cease their fighting, loudly announce that they will each receive a third check after their names, which means they will be expelled and their parents will be notified.
5. Call in professionals: If they do not cease their fighting, loudly announce that you are calling the police. As fifty percent of combatants will not respond to the previous steps, it is important at this point to turn the problem over to professionals trained in handling violence.

There are several problems with this system, of course. One is that both participants would be seriously injured or dead by the time the scenario played out. Another is that it ignores the role of intuition and robs teachers of their professional initiative to do what they know needs to be done.

## SCHÖN AND WORLDMAKING

According to Schön, the modernist curriculum removes individual cognition from its social base. "'Knowing that' tends to take priority over 'knowing how'; and know-how, when it does make its appearance, takes the form of science-based technique."[6] Teaching in this model is merely transferring information; learning is simply receiving, storing, and repeating information. This makes good television quiz show contestants but not good professionals. Although professional education focuses on the cognitive aspects of learning a profession, Schön describes working professionals as drawing primarily from an unconscious process that results from the actual performing of professional work; this is an implicit knowledge that they use but don't understand.

> Often we cannot say what it is that we know. When we try to describe it we find ourselves at a loss, or we produce descriptions that are obviously inappropriate. Our knowing is ordinarily tacit, implicit in our patterns of action and in our feel for the stuff with which we are dealing. It seems right to say that our knowing is in our action.[7]

He emphasizes the paradox involved when master practitioners attempt to teach students, in which students are unable to understand what they are supposed to learn, and teachers cannot explain why the truths they know are true. Using the example of an architectural design student to anchor his observations, Schön observes:

> Initially, the student does not and cannot understand what designing means. He finds the artistry of thinking like an architect to be elusive, obscure, alien, and mysterious. . . . From his observation of the students' performance, the studio master realizes that they do not at first understand the essential things. He sees, further, that he cannot explain these things with any hope of being understood, at least at the onset, because they can be grasped only through the experience of actual designing.[8]

For Schön, although the most important aspects of professional education cannot be taught, they can be learned. Teachers cannot make students see things; students need to learn to see things on their own. The role of the teachers is not to teach, but to guide by creating relevant learning experiences. Anything worth learning can only be learned *indirectly* through a learning experience that requires learners to do something they will not be able to understand until it has already been accomplished.

It is as though the studio master had said to him, "I can tell you that there is something you need to know, and with my help you may be able to understand it. But I cannot tell you what it is in a way that you can now understand it. I can only arrange for you to have the right sorts of experiences for yourself. You must be willing, therefore, to have these experiences. Then you will be able to make an informed choice about whether you wish to continue. If you are unwilling to step into this new experience without knowing ahead of time what it will be like, I cannot help you. You must trust me."[9]

The teacher can help students to realize what they have learned after the learning has occurred. This practice of urging a student to "reflect" on what learning has taken place is the essence of Schön's notion of *reflective practice*.

Schön writes in several places that the student must be willing to learn and must trust the teacher. The demands of real learning cause the prospective learner to feel uncertain, anxious, and even angry. Especially in our culture, which has been deceived into believing education should be easy and painless, real learning often causes intense frustration. We seem satisfied with *having* an education rather than *being* educated. We are willing to collect and use information, but we don't want to risk real change, which often forces significant adjustment in our lives. We have come to expect comfortable education; course evaluations are often statements of our comfort levels rather than our learning. Uncomfortable education requires that students begin to trust their teachers. We will shortly examine the wisdom of Schön's call for *trust*.

Schön also helps us understand the social roots of individual learning. As we get to the design level, Schön illustrates how accomplished practitioners guide students through a vocabulary and a meaning system that the teacher takes for granted and the student finds either confusing or incomprehensible.

Through countless acts of attention and inattention, naming, sensemaking, boundary setting, and control, they make and maintain the worlds matched to their professional knowledge and know-how.[10]

The important thing that is being transmitted, according to Schön, is not the informational knowledge but the world view of the teacher and the discipline. Schön cites professor Thomas Cowan saying, "law school, I discovered, primarily trains students to listen . . . to think and talk in the way the rest of the profession does."[11] Once the teacher's world construction has been successfully transmitted to the student, the emulation of that practice is painless and the knowledge is obvious. Traweek, in her study of physicists and their apprentices, reinforces the views of Kuhn and Schön.

> Novices must learn what sorts of things they need to know to be taken seriously; they must become unselfconscious practitioners of the culture, feeling the appropriate desires and anxieties, thinking about the world in a characteristic way. . . . [Physicists] are bound together by a way of thinking, about the world and about knowledge and about themselves.[12]

This constructed world view of the discipline extends beyond the professional culture, influencing an individual's view of the larger society. The same combinations of attention and inattention that bind together a profession tend to create parallel constructions outside the profession. Marketers have long known that professional association exerts a key influence on such things as the kind of car a person drives, the kind of clothes a person wears, and whether someone will contribute to public radio.

We forget how our various social groupings have influenced learning that we now take for granted. I became very aware of this one night at a college play. Many of the faculty with whom I worked attended an enjoyable student comedy one Saturday evening. During the intermission, I noticed a student from one of my classes and asked him how he was enjoying the production. He gave an answer I didn't expect. He said, "I saw this play on Thursday night, too, since it was free to students. I have to tell you that I'm enjoying it a lot more tonight with so many of the faculty here." When I asked why, he answered, "Because the faculty knows where to laugh." I never considered that students learned where to laugh by attending plays with people who did (who had learned to laugh by attending plays with people who did). This should not really have been so surprising to me, given the universality of "laugh tracks" on television comedies, but his statement stuck with me. It is stunning in its own way that one of the things college students learn to do is to laugh in the right places. I somehow doubt that anyone thought to include this in a curriculum.

## WORLD VIEW LOSS

The acquisition of a different world view is a difficult process for both students and teachers. In opening up to a different world view, students take a significant risk, experiencing a sense of loss at leaving behind world views in which they already know the rules, and sometimes leaving behind people with whom they shared those world views.

> What makes this situation into a predicament for the student is that he or she is likely to find the costs of commitment greater than its expected rewards. . . . Swimming in unfamiliar waters, the student risks the loss of his sense of competence, control, and confidence. He must temporarily abandon much that he already values. If he comes to the studio with knowledge he considers useful, he may be asked to unlearn it. . . . And he may fear that, by a kind of insidious coercion, he may permanently lose what he already knows and values.[13]

Because students are risking a great deal, they will be able to embrace new world views only if they make "a leap of faith"[14] and are "capable of the willing suspension of disbelief."[15]

A student's present cultural role can provide resistance to the adoption of a new role. Ebaugh highlights the cost involved in changing social roles. As one role is typically left behind in order to adopt a new one, any role change threatens self-identity. Ebaugh has studied role change in people who have left all different kinds of roles behind to adopt new ones, including ex-nuns, ex-doctors, ex-prostitutes, recovering alcoholics, divorcees, widows, retirees, and transsexuals. She noted that role exiters initially question their present roles and deliberately explore the costs and rewards of changing roles. They tend to consciously accept a new role only after experiencing some sort of turning point that involves personal support for the change. Once that turning point is reached, exiters work diligently to establish a new identity. Until this process is complete, the new identity is held tentatively, at arm's length.

## LOOKING IN THE SAME DIRECTION

Schön also discusses the time required to accomplish immersion into a new world view. In our fast-paced, instant culture, there is an increasing push to press the element of time out of learning as impatient "customers" try to buy their educations. In P–12 schools, the emphasis is on learning everything earlier and faster. In universities, schools are under tremendous pressure to package curricula so they can be covered in shorter and shorter periods of time. Down deep, we all know it takes time to learn things well. On the surface, we often pretend this isn't true in order to fill our classrooms and keep cash-hungry institutions afloat.

Here too, Schön provides us with a valuable insight. The reason time is important is because we teachers are transmitting much more than surface knowledge. It takes time to transmit an entire world view; it takes time to acquire and accept a whole different way of being. It takes time to see things differently. It takes time because it is indirect; it is between the lines. It can't be placed in a syllabus and directly taught and evaluated. In fact, in the way we view teaching in this book, it can't be taught at all— it can only be learned. A friend of mine, known for his pithy, interesting insights, told me that the best conversations he has with his son "are when they are both looking in the same direction."

Implied here is something many of us know intuitively—some things need to be addressed indirectly. It is easier to talk about some issues indirectly while focusing directly on another task. I was aware as an English teacher that conversations I had with students that seemed to be about literature or writing were often about other adolescent issues bouncing around inside of them, issues that they were not able to talk about directly. I always pitied the school counselors who had no context in which to discuss things indirectly. Direct approaches often yield very little because they encounter direct resistance. Change isn't easy. Schön demonstrates that while students and teachers are together involved in such subjects as design, they are both looking in the same direction, teaching and learning things that can't be taught. It takes time to learn this way, since it isn't neat and orderly.

Students do not so much attend these events as live in them. And the work of a reflective practicum takes a long time. Indeed, nothing is so indicative of progress in the acquisition of artistry as the student's discovery of the time it takes—time to live through the initial shocks of confusion and mystery, unlearn initial expectations and begin to master the practice of the practicum, time to live through the learning cycles involved in any design-like task; and time to shift repeatedly back and forth between reflection on and in action.[16]

The issue of time also works together with the issue of loss and trust. Time is an indicator of the level of willingness to immerse oneself in a discipline; it is an indicator of willingness to go beyond the minimum, to play, and to have fun. We are not willing to commit significant time to activities to which we have not fully committed. Stephen King writes of this in his advice to aspiring writers. He describes how he knew it was time to discontinue his son Owen's saxophone lessons seven months after starting them.

> I knew, not because Owen stopped practicing, but because he was practicing only during the periods Mr. Bowie had set for him: half an hour after school four days a week, plus an hour on weekends. . . . And as soon as his practice time was over, it was back into the case with the horn, and there it stayed until the next lesson or practice time. What this suggested to me was that when it came to the sax and my son, there was never going to be any real play-time; it was all going to be rehearsal. That's no good. If there's no joy in it, it's just no good. It's best to go on to some other area, where the deposits of talent may be richer and the fun quotient higher.[17]

King brings out a crucial point here. People will commit the time necessary to master any kind of task only if they can find an innate joy in that activity, only if it becomes a type of play. Until that point, a person is simply testing out a role and walking around the periphery of a discipline. The fear of loss, not enough commitment, and not enough time hinder world view acquisition. These important points reappear in a resounding way later in this book.

## Building on Schön

Lévi-Strauss wrote, "for each scholar and each writer, the particular way he or she thinks and writes opens a new outlook on mankind."[18] So after acknowledging my debt to Schön, I need to move with it in a different direction. Schön provides a spectacular, innovative perspective on the problem of teaching and learning and lays the groundwork for an intriguing solution. After laying out a compelling argument for the importance of world view acquisition in professional education, Schön launches into his reflective practice model as the way to make world view acquisition conscious. What Schön doesn't do adequately, however, is to explain how world view acquisition actually occurs. What is being acquired, and how does one acquire it? He describes it vaguely as a by-product of professional activity. His solution is to employ reflective techniques to extract what has been learned from one's "knowing in action." I was dissatisfied with this aspect of his argument and sought a better answer. It is here that the fields of sociology and anthropology were very helpful.

## RITUAL AND MYTH

### Emile Durkheim

The ideas of sociologist Emile Durkheim help us to understand how a world view is transmitted. It must be noted that Durkheim's ideas were much more complex than they will appear in the following paragraphs; I would direct readers interested in a more thorough depiction of Durkheimian theory on this topic to the journal article by Rigoni and LaMagdeleine listed in this book's bibliography. For the purposes of this book, I believe that my simplified depiction of his thinking remains faithful to the basic premises of his work.

Durkheim was interested in how social groups formed and achieved solidarity.[19] He proposed that social groups were created and maintained through the sharing of sacred myth and sacred ritual.[20] He initially found that less technological societies were held together by strong religious elements. In such societies, social roles tended to be fixed, with all members performing similar tasks. In a traditional society, religion served as a type of sacred glue that held each society together through universal participation in established religious rituals and myths.

As technology increases, social roles tend to diversify and individuals tend to specialize in tasks not performed by others. Obvious examples in our society are subdividing medical doctors into a plethora of specialties and teachers into many disciplines and licenses. Durkheim argued that in this more diverse technological society, the general glue to hold the larger society together weakens and is replaced by the cohesion of smaller, specialized workplace groups that join to support general social principles. Durkheim developed a historically derived argument that members of work groups could well share quasi-religious beliefs about the world. These beliefs convey basic assumptions about behaviors and attitudes, just as traditional religion has previously done for entire societies.[21] As an example, Durkheim wrote that "teachers must convey a deep respect for both the subject matter and the rules of evidence that undergird both science and modern law."[22]

Durkheim maintained that in any body of collective representations, including those among strong work cultures, one subset is considered sacred. Like traditional religious accounts, occupational culture relies on embedded (sacred) moral premises that serve as yardsticks for how to conduct our lives. For Durkheim, the acquisition of professional morality requires the same kind of internalization that occurs through participation in religious rituals and through the telling of sacred stories. Over time and through the emulation of routinized activities, an aspirant learns how a "professional" views reality.

> Social groups would develop and reinforce these group moral accounts the same way that sacred representations have always been developed—with the use of powerful symbols, mythic collective stories, and (especially) rituals. To the extent that they represent the importance of a group, its distinguishing technologies, and its cardinal operating premises, these accounts amount to a set of moral representations about it.[23]

There are clues as to what is sacred within a group. Something is usually sacred if it is capable of evoking group anger when it is not treated with "proper respect" and when the disrespect is undertaken behind a cloak of secrecy and subterfuge. As an undergraduate English major, I once witnessed the breaking of a sacred English department precept. Several of us complained one day that the poetry we were reading was obscure and vague. We were certain that poets like T. S. Eliot were putting us on by writing obscure images, passing it off as great art, and laughing at us behind our backs. (Our certainty demonstrated the proof of Schön's assertion that apprentices look with suspicion upon the teachings of their professors.)

One group member, Ross, was a budding poet who, with several poetry publications already to his name, was respected and held in awe by the rest of us. Ross decided to conjure up the most outrageous images he could contrive, put them together as a poem, and submit it to the student literary magazine under a pseudonym. I have forgotten all but one colorful phrase from his submission. It read, "Peanut butter on doorknobs crushing lice," and it typified the rest of the poem. It was deposited in the in-basket of the magazine under the pseudonym of Bill Jordan.

This prank turned into an attack on the sacred fabric of the university when one of the faculty advisors to the magazine read the poem—and loved it. He didn't recall having ever met Bill Jordan, so he went to the registrar's office to locate his phone number. He was very eager to talk with this gifted young poet. But the poet could not be located despite the teacher's efforts, and eventually the truth emerged. The faculty member slowly realized he had been duped; he was very embarrassed, and he was very, very angry. Ross grew very quiet, and he became very, very careful. Without other solid support from within the faculty, Ross might have needed to switch schools.

Ross had made a fool of a faculty member by desecrating late twentieth century poetry. He exposed the weakness of the automatic and uncritical postmodern acceptance of random bizarre imagery as great art. We didn't know then that not everyone was a T. S. Eliot, and not everyone was a Picasso. Ross's prank exposed the fact that not all faculty were aware of this either. Toying with the sacred is a dangerous thing.

Academics have long recognized the reality of group socialization and have paid much attention to such things as dress, grooming, and etiquette acculturation. What we are looking at here builds on this idea but goes far beyond it by including more comprehensive epistemological and moral components. Although socialization bestows a certain cultural sophistication within a group, Durkheim argues that ritual and myth alert group members to what is sacred within that group. We are at the point of recognizing that an entire collective consciousness (world view or paradigm) needs to be transmitted, accepted, and integrated with each new member of a group. This requires the deep internalization resulting from intense participation in captivating group rituals and from the recitation of powerful group myths. The myths and rituals transmit the sacred between-the-lines elements of the collective consciousness on which participants rely despite their inability to recognize or articulate this knowledge. The repetition of these rituals creates a unique view of reality in an aspiring professional and helps mature members of a profession stay grounded within the group.[24]

It is important to note at this point that rituals need not be lavish formal events, and myths need not be distant tribal stories. For Durkheim, a ritual is a way of focusing a student's attention and emotions, and a myth is a way of transmitting certain expectations. Rituals transmit societal and cultural meanings symbolically. Peter McLaren points out that the words on any page that were chosen to develop ideas are themselves part of a ritual event. McLaren also quotes Ronald Grimes, who said, "Pen and paper are power objects, fetishes; theorizing and observing are ritual gestures laden with ideology."[25]

## The Urinal Game

I receive a lot of humorous e-mail from friends around the country. One of the items I received some time ago was something called "The Urinal Game," a little program created by a company called Clever Media. The opening screen of the programs says, "The object of the game is to test your knowledge of men's room etiquette. You will be presented with several scenarios. In each you must select the proper urinal etiquette." Each scenario features a row of six urinals and a door: ① ② ③ ④ ⑤ ⑥ [Door]. I will describe a few of the scenarios here:

*Scenario A:* ① ② ③ ④ ⑤ ⑥ *[Door]*

Urinal #1 is occupied. This one is simple for any veteran urinal user. The correct choice for someone entering the room is urinal #6. The player is informed that the underlying principles behind this choice are those of "maximum buffer zone" and "respect for personal space."

*Scenario B:* ① ② ③ ④ ⑤ ⑥ *[Door]*

Urinals #3 and #4 are occupied. The correct choice for someone entering the room is urinal #1. The rule here is to be furthest from the door to shield your personal space from door traffic.

*Scenario C:* ① ② ③ ④ ⑤ ⑥ *[Door]*

Urinals #1, #3, and #5 are occupied. The correct choice for someone entering the room is urinal #6. The rule here is less obvious. Although you end up standing next to the door and dealing with door traffic, it is better to stand next to one person than between two people. The program reminds the player, "Don't forget to keep your eyes on the wall in front of you."

*Scenario D:* ① ② ③ ④ ⑤ ⑥ *[Door]*

Urinals #2, #5, and #6 are occupied. The person at #2 is a very large person. This is a more subtle choice—the correct choice for someone entering the room is urinal #4. The rule here is, Don't stand next to the big guy ("People might think that you and the big guy are pairing up if you use one of the urinals next to him.").

And, finally,

*Scenario E:* ① ② ③ ④ ⑤ ⑥ *[Door]*

Urinals #2, #4, and #6 are occupied. This is, perhaps, the most interesting scenario. The only correct choice is to leave and return later, as there is no good option here. I have actually observed individuals doing this in real life.

The amusing Urinal Game is also quite instructive. All the males I know who have played this game get most of the scenarios correct (some miss on scenario E; I believe it is because they think they need to make a choice and do not know they can go back out the door). It is instructive because it makes us aware of unwritten rules and the fact that we have learned them somewhere without being aware that we had done so. In fact, we learned them through ritual and myth. Men have learned them from the verbal and nonverbal correction of parents, from the taunts of adolescent hazing, from discreetly observing others' behavior in rest rooms. We are also dimly aware of the mainly homophobic myths that underlie these rituals. Rest room behavior is a realm in which males learn many of the boundaries of their social relationships with other men. Much of the remainder of the sacred moral code governing male relationships builds on the fundamental lessons of bathroom behavior—buffer zones and respect for personal space govern much male–male behavior. Durkheim's assertion that we learn through ritual and myth is brought home in a simple (albeit trite) example. Others have built on Durkheim's insights.

## Erving Goffman

Goffman reinforced and expanded the idea that cultural communication occurs indirectly and unconsciously, stating that the observer, "as well as his subjects, tends to take the framework of everyday life for granted; he remains unaware of what guides him and them."[26] Goffman used the terms *frame* and *framework* to refer to the principles of organization that govern social events and our subjective involvement in them.

> Social frameworks . . . provide background understanding for events that incorporate the will, aim, and controlling effort of an intelligence, a live agency, the chief one being the human being.[27]

A variety of frames provide the context within which any specific statement, question, or action is interpreted. These presuppositions are, in fact, essential to understanding any utterance. The physical act of raising a hand in the air may indicate a vote, a salute, a greeting, or a request to be recognized at a meeting. It is the socially prescribed meaning that determines the significance of the gesture.

> [Goffman] believed that our observations are understandable only in terms of the frame we put around them. Frames answer the question "What is happening here?"; they tell us how to define the situations in which we find ourselves. Frames provide a way of organizing our experiences. Without them, the social world is only a chaotic abundance of facts.[28]

Goffman was aware that his ideas could lend themselves to a totally relativist viewpoint in which nothing has any meaning outside of the frame. Goffman used the concept of a *primary* framework to counter this relativism: "a primary framework is one that is seen as rendering what would otherwise be a meaningless aspect of the scene into something that is meaningful."[29] Collins gets more specific. "What is the core, the primary frame, as Goffman puts it? It is the real physical world and the real social presence of human bodies within it."[30] McLaren, like Schön, critiques the modernist separation of mind and body that ignores anything but cognitive knowledge. In Durkheimian terms, this separation is a major myth in the quasi religion of science.

> The ritualized practices of school research have, throughout history, overlooked the fact that the body plays an important part in the acquisition of knowledge.[31]

From this perspective, Goffman's views are a direct attack on the relativistic view that society is a group of individual realities without any authoritative glue. Collins describes Goffman's perspective as one of social realism.

> [Garfinkel insists] that everything is locally produced, that there are no general laws at all. [Goffman] attacks this view, insisting that there is an overall social structure and we can make valid generalizations about it. Even within any situation, the talk and the cognitive constructions are not primary, but only part of a set of embedded frames. The largest frame is the physical world and the bodies of the people interacting in it performing Durkheimian rituals.[32]

Most people have heard the joke about the two psychiatrists who meet in the hall on the way to their offices one morning. One psychiatrist says to the other, "Good morning." The second psychiatrist mutters to himself, "I wonder what he meant by that?" Psychological matters aside, Goffman might well comment on this exchange. Saying "good morning" is indeed a ritual exchange, and it does convey various things depending on the frame in which it is embedded.

While I was still teaching high school, Brian, a former student stopped by to visit one day. My class had just ended and, with my one prep hour just beginning, I asked him to walk with me to the faculty lounge so we could visit. As we walked through the halls, I exchanged greetings with a steady stream of students who were switching classes: Hi, Mr. Rigoni. Hi, Jennifer. Hi, Mr. Rigoni. Hi, Chris. Mr. Rigoni! John! It continued. Then as we turned a corner, there was: Hi, Mr. Rigoni. Hi, Oscar. At this, Brian said to me, "He's one of your basketball players, isn't he?" I answered that he was and asked Brian how he knew this. (Oscar was no more than 5′9″.) His answer was simple: "Your voice conveyed a special hello for him."

Something as simple as a greeting conveys a great deal of information. Instead of psychiatrists, consider a school building where a cafeteria worker and the building principal pass each other in the hall. What are the implications if they pass, look at each other, and continue walking without saying anything? What are the implications if the cafeteria worker says "good morning" and the principal says nothing? What are the implications if the principal says, "Good morning, Hazel" and the cafeteria worker says, "Mornin', Dr. Fishbreath"? Each of these scenarios frames things about the two actors and their relationship to each other. These scenarios frame deeper social relationships, including personal respect, professional roles, self-image, and especially, power.

## Mary Douglas

Mary Douglas describes how the culture of modern institutions affects the process of social cognition.[33] She distinguishes social cognition from individual cognition by describing how social institutions delimit the cognition by controlling analogies, conferring identities, and determining what will be remembered and what will be forgotten. She uses a Durkheimian viewpoint to demonstrate that professionalization, beyond the formal knowledge and skills, is learning what to remember and to forget, learning what to see, learning how to frame what is seen, and learning how to apply all of the above. Sounding much like Schön, she indicates that knowing how to identify and use relevant knowledge is more important than simply having the knowledge. Oakes's study of life insurance agents concretely demonstrates Douglas's theoretical perspective.[34] He shows that the culture of agents, developed through training and supported with rewards and punishments, is intended to reconstruct agents' entire views of life, not just their approaches to work itself.

## The Myth of Family

At the start of my second year at a small private college, I attended the beginning-of-the-year barbeque for faculty and staff. It was set up to emulate a large family picnic, with food, games, and superficial conversation. I worked my way through the food line and ended up at the point where, in a symbolic show of equalitarian goodwill, hamburgers and bratwurst were transferred from the grill to the bun of your choice by the college president and the dean. Attempting to make small talk with them, I said innocently (and, as it turns out, stupidly), "There are a lot of people here I don't know. We must have had quite a few people leave last year." To that, both the president and the dean simultaneously shouted, "No, we didn't!" The anger in their voices made me think immediately of my grandmother's farm and the feeling of stepping in something I shouldn't have. I slid away, determined to find an explanation for their reaction. In the next few years, I became aware of the concepts of institutional mythology and ritual, and I formed a tentative explanation that was confirmed at a gathering for yet another group of new faculty. On this occasion at the president's home, I heard the president's wife repeat no fewer than four times: "Every year we have lots of new faculty, but no one ever leaves." The repetition assured me that this was the key to the myth.

In retrospect, the barbeque ritual was intended to affect the feeling of a happy family picnic. The president and the dean were playing the role of family patriarchs while promoting an illusion of equalitarianism by personally distributing food to "lesser" family members. This led to the main myth, one of the most sacred myths of the institution—many people joined this wonderful family, but no one ever left. This was slightly modified in subsequent years when it became obvious that people did indeed leave the family. The modification added that people never left the family unless something was wrong with them. People who left were flawed. At the institutional level, they simply disappeared. They were seldom mentioned again in official conversation; if they were mentioned, it was inevitably a negative reference that stated that their replacements were vastly superior to them. The only people who left and remained in the institutional consciousness were people who were very well liked and who left due to some special circumstance such as a spouse transfer. This was akin to a relative leaving the area due to marriage. Once or twice someone left and returned and, like the biblical prodigal child, was lavishly welcomed back. The story about what a mistake it had been to leave was widely repeated; they had now seen the light and had returned. This was the way the institution controlled key perceptions.

## WHAT I LEARNED

So what had I learned in all this reading and research? I learned about worldmaking. I learned that, philosophically and even scientifically, reality wasn't as real as I had once thought. I learned that the belief that reality was fixed and objectively open to appropriate scientific techniques was a problematic and outdated world view. I learned that constructivism maintained that what we call *reality* is a cultural construction. With the rise of other less positivistic views of science has come the understanding that science itself is a constructed reality. If science is a constructed reality and a student wishes to be a scientist, the task at hand for that student is to construct a scientific world view. Capital R "Reality" is too huge and complex for us to experience directly. Every group has a constructed reality. To be able to thrive in any group culture depends on our ability to adopt the reality construction of that group. All reality constructions are viewed as the one and only reality and are therefore invisible to those who hold them.

I learned that Schön offers us an important alternative view of learning. He says that anything worth learning cannot be directly taught. However, it can be learned. The role of a teacher is to set up situations to help students learn what the teacher knows but cannot directly teach. Students can only learn these important things indirectly, through a transformation of vision. To transform their vision, students need to trust the teacher, to be completely willing to alter their world views, and to dedicate the necessary time to complete this transformation. Schön does not, however, offer any actual insight as to how this transformation of vision actually occurs.

I learned that Durkheim proposes that the transformation of vision is a quasi-religious experience. Vision is transformed by indirectly learning the sacred assumptions of a culture through the participation in cultural rituals and the transmission of its imbedded mythology. Goffman further developed the Durkheimian idea of indirect communication through social ritual with his concept of cultural frames, which determine the meaning of any given act. And finally, Douglas demonstrates that organizations and professions use ritual and myth to influence the world views of individual members.

As I again asked myself my original questions about teaching, I was struck by the huge gulf between what I had learned and how education is currently practiced. I formed several assumptions:

First, our best students are students who have assimilated the world view of our disciplines; our average students have assimilated some aspects of it but have missed (or resisted) other aspects; our worst students have largely missed (or resisted) the world view completely.

Second, existing curricula and pedagogy do help our best students to modify their world views; they do not help others. The popular myth that some get it and some don't is very accurate. This is true in large degree because our curricula and pedagogy only haphazardly influence world view change.

Third, education, as developed through a modernist perspective, has focused on a curriculum that introduces the right information in the right way at the right time. How the information is organized is deemed important; when it is taught is deemed important. Information is the key to the process. It is a teacher's job to present this important information; it is the student's primary duty to memorize and regurgitate it. As a modernist process, this is largely described as straightforward, even technical.

Finally, more students, not just the very adept and very fortunate, would be successful if we understood that our primary purpose in education was worldmaking and if we used techniques to expedite worldmaking. We need to do consciously and purposefully what we now do unconsciously and accidentally. The next chapter offers one such approach to consider.

## NOTES

1. Thomas S. Kuhn, *The Structure of Scientific Revolutions,* 2d ed. (Chicago: University of Chicago Press, 1970), 112.

2. Martin Goldstein and Inge F. Goldstein, *How We Know: An Exploration of the Scientific Process* (New York: Plenum, 1978), 21.

3. Donald A. Schön, *Educating the Reflective Practitioner: Toward a New Design in Teaching and Learning in the Professions* (San Francisco, Calif.: Jossey-Bass, 1987), 3.

4. Schön, *Educating,* 11.

5. Schön, *Educating,* 13.

6. Schön, *Educating,* 309.

7. Donald A. Schön, *The Reflective Practitioner: How Professionals Think in Action* (San Francisco, Calif.: Basic Books, 1983), 49.

8. Schön, *Educating,* 82.

9. Schön, *Educating,* 93.

10. Schön, *Educating*, 36.

11. Schön, *Educating*, 92–93.

12. Sharon Traweek, *Beamtimes and Lifetimes: The World of High Energy Physicists* (Cambridge: Harvard University Press, 1988), xi.

13. Schön, *Educating*, 94–95.

14. Schön, *Educating*, 85.

15. Schön, *Educating*, 94.

16. Schön, *Educating*, 311.

17. Stephen King, *On Writing: A Memoir of the Craft* (New York: Pocket Books, 2000), 149–150.

18. Claude Lévi-Strauss, *Myth and Meaning: Cracking the Code of Culture* (1978; reprint, New York: Schocken Books, 1995), 4.

19. Emile Durkheim, *The Division of Labor in Society*, trans. George Simpson (1893; reprint, New York: Free Press, 1933).

20. Emile Durkheim, *The Elementary Forms of the Religious Life* (1915; reprint, New York: Free Press, 1965).

21. Emile Durkheim, *Professional Ethics and Civic Morals* (New York: Routledge, 1957).

22. David P. Rigoni and Donald R. LaMagdeleine, "Computer Majors' Education as Moral Enterprise: A Durkheimian Analysis," *Journal of Moral Education* 27, no. 4 (December 1998): 490.

23. Rigoni and LaMagdeleine, "Moral Enterprise," 491.

24. Rigoni and LaMagdeleine, "Moral Enterprise," 491.

25. Peter McLaren, *Schooling as a Ritual Performance: Toward A Political Economy of Educational Symbols and Gestures* (New York: Routledge, 1993), 37.

26. Erving Goffman, *Frame Analysis: An Essay on the Organization of Experience* (Boston: Northeast University Press, 1974), 564.

27. Goffman, *Frame Analysis*, 22.

28. Philip Manning, *Erving Goffman and Modern Sociology* (Stanford, Calif.: Stanford University Press, 1992), 118.

29. Goffman, *Frame Analysis*, 21.

30. Randall Collins, *Three Sociological Traditions* (New York: Oxford University Press, 1985), 218.

31. Collins, *Traditions*, 221.

32. Collins, *Traditions*, 225.

33. Mary Douglas, *How Institutions Think* (Syracuse, N.Y.: Syracuse University Press, 1986).

34. Guy Oakes, *The Soul of the Salesman: The Moral Ethos of Personal Sales* (Atlantic Highlands, N.J.: Humanities Press International, 1990).

# Chapter Four

# The Shaman's Strategy

"The world is a mystery," he said. "And it is not at all as you picture it."—Don Juan

> Carlos Castaneda, *Journey to Ixtlan: The Lessons of Don Juan*
> (New York: Pocket Books, 1974), 165.

"All of us go through the same shenanigans," he said after a long pause. "The only way to overcome them is to persist in acting like a warrior. The rest comes of itself and by itself."

"What is the rest, don Juan?"

"Knowledge and power. Men of knowledge have both. And yet none of them could tell how they got to have them, except that they had kept on acting like warriors and at a given moment everything changed."

> Carlos Castaneda, *Journey to Ixtlan: The Lessons of Don Juan*
> (New York: Pocket Books, 1974), 165.

Up to this point, I had learned a lot. At various points, the philosophical and scientific viewpoints appeared to reinforce each other. Constructivist philosophy maintains that although a universal reality may exist, we are not able to comprehend that reality in its entirety and, therefore, we construct a reality through our acceptance of various portions of the whole. Modern physics demonstrates that even from the perspective of hard science, reality is a very slippery concept. Therefore, physics discusses reality in terms of probability rather than certainty. Durkheim, Schön, and others provide other important thinking about ritual, myth, and educational worldview transformation. Yet, at this point in my research, theory alone was becoming tedious, and I needed to see how all these ideas fit the actual practice of teaching and learning. I needed to see *how* ritual and mythology could help a teacher facilitate the invisible transformation of someone's world view. The practical application of this process became apparent one day as I read a book written by controversial anthropologist Carlos Castaneda, who had written a series of books about his initiation into the world of a Yaqui Indian shaman. Castaneda initiated my interest in the shaman as an expert in altering world views.

> The word *shaman* (pronounced SHAH-maan) is a word from the language of the Tungus people of Siberia and has been adapted widely by anthropologists to refer to persons in a great variety of non-Western cultures who were previously known by such terms as "witch," "witch-doctor," "medicine man," "sorcerer," "wizard," "magic man," "magician," and "seer." One of the advantages of using the term is that it lacks the prejudicial overtones and conflicting meanings associated with more familiar labels. . . . A shaman is a man or woman who enters an altered state of consciousness—at will—to contact and utilize an ordinarily hidden reality in order to acquire knowledge and power, and to help other persons.[1]

Why utilize a metaphor so obviously foreign to our Western culture? Walter Goldschmidt, in his foreword to Castaneda's first book, offers an interesting explanation.

> The central importance of entering into worlds other than our own—and hence of anthropology itself—lies in the fact that the experience leads us to understand that our own world is also a cultural construct. By experiencing other worlds, then, we see our own for what it is and are thereby enabled also to see fleetingly what the real world, the one between our own cultural construct and those other worlds, must in fact be like.[2]

His viewpoint supports a basic task of this book, which argues that the most important aspect of education involves the unobserved learning that changes a student's world view. The shaman perspective provides a natural connection, as the fundamental focus of a shaman's teaching is a purposeful change in the world view of an apprentice. Although teachers at all levels of contemporary education help some students adjust and change their world views, what separates a shaman from an ordinary teacher is that a shaman is *intentional* in effecting that change.

The world view changes that do occur in most contemporary educational settings tend to be accidental (or at least incidental), while rapt attention is afforded to what is actually the peripheral means to that end. This book will use a teacher-as-shaman metaphor to argue that what is (at worst) absent and (at best) implicit and unconscious in contemporary education needs to be made explicit and conscious, and what is currently thought to be an end product is, in actuality, merely an intermediate step to this end.

## CONTROVERSIAL CASTANEDA

Heated controversy surrounds the anthropological work of Carlos Castaneda. His books describe his alleged initiation into the world view of a Yaqui Indian sorcerer he identifies as *don Juan Mateus*. Castaneda's third book, *Journey to Ixtlan*, was based on his 1973 Ph.D. dissertation in anthropology at UCLA. Supporters take Castaneda's conversations with his teacher, don Juan, as factual, despite his unwillingness to offer proof of their authenticity. Detractors view his writings as a hoax and accuse Castaneda of writing little more than entertaining novels. Despite the presence of such noted scholars as Harold Garfinkel on Castaneda's dissertation committee, the controversy has continued through the years. At one level, the academic critique of his work is simply a legitimate critical assessment. At another level, there is much in the critique that is simply vicious and mean-spirited. It is obvious that Castaneda stomped on some sacred ground and that this sacred ground has been vigorously defended with an emotion reserved for the defense of sacred principles. The result is a complex, tangled, and controversial argument.

I intend to discuss the main arguments of the Castaneda debate and to offer an explanation of why I make use of his work despite the controversy. I include this section for those who are inclined to wade into academic debates. Such readers might dismiss the key ideas of this book if I proceeded without such a discussion. Readers who are interested in such a discussion should simply continue reading. Readers who are not interested in such a discussion may continue the practice established earlier in the book; they may feel free to skip this discussion and jump ahead to the section entitled "Don Juan's Sorcery."

Richard de Mille, Castaneda's self-appointed debunker, reflects both the rational academic arguments and the less rational defense of the sacred. He argues that Castaneda's work is fiction created not from field research but from the ideas and words of others. Specifically, he contends that Castaneda's field reports contradict each other, that his writing lacks convincing detail and includes implausible detail, and that the words of other writers emerge from don Juan's mouth.[3] De Mille describes Castaneda's work as valid but inauthentic, valid because it corresponds with what is known, inauthentic because it does not (in his view) arise from actual field work.[4]

There is also an acidic edge to de Mille's critique. For example, he exceeded the normal bounds of academic analysis when he wrote to the Library of Congress's Director of Cataloging and criticized the library's designation of Castaneda's writings as legitimate anthropological work.[5] This edge is also displayed in his biting satires (he claims to be unable to write without utilizing "humor"), with which he works to discredit Castaneda without the use of rational argument. Stephen Murray legitimates this type of satirical scorn as being necessary whenever a group of scientists embrace "poor science." He does not delve into the question of which scientists get to determine which research is poor science or which group gets to coerce another into group-think conformity. Of Castaneda's work, he says:

> I have argued that ignoring what is regarded as poor science is standard procedure in all scientific disciplines. Only when suspect work does not disappear from *scientific* discourse, when it is taken seriously by some *scientists*, does scientific scorn become visible. . . . When informal organized skepticism failed to kill the work within the discipline, public discussion became necessary.[6]

It is, perhaps, easier and more honest to depict this as an age-old technique of intimidation into mainstream conformance and of instilling in potential mavericks the intimation of becoming the next scornful target.

Others besides de Mille are critical of Castaneda's work. Southwestern desert expert Hans Sebald criticizes the flora, fauna, and climate of the Sonoran desert described by Castaneda as mere literary inventions.

> While almost any one of these environmental anomalies could arise from poor observation or unusual circumstances, the accumulation of many such

incongruities conclusively disauthenticates the setting of Castaneda's purported field work.[7]

Richard McDermott feels that although Castaneda can be valuably read as fiction, he fails to use literary devices to inform readers that the writings are meant to be read as nonfiction; this presents problems in assessing the authenticity of his writing.[8]

Paul Reisman provides a thoughtful critique that echoes the ambivalence of many dealing with Castaneda. "To be quite honest," he writes, " I have been confused; I have just not known what to think about Castaneda."[9] He expresses comfort in don Juan's postmodern, constructivist view of reality.

> according to don Juan neither the sorcerer's view nor the normal view *is* reality. Whatever is actually out there can in fact not be perceived, because to perceive is to create an image out of the meanings we have acquired by growing up as social beings. Ultimate reality does exist; it is what is there when we stop perceiving the world, that is, when we utterly stop telling ourselves what it is we are seeing.[10]

Then he moves beyond comfort and expresses the nagging discomfort he has had with the works of Castaneda. He cites Castaneda's "deliberate blurring" of the line between science and literature as the source of this discomfort. "By writing in such a way as to transform an anthropological study into a fictional genre, Castaneda employs our deeply held confidence in the truth of science to make us doubt that same truth."[11]

Several professors, friends, and acquaintances from Castaneda's UCLA days seem convinced that, at least in the beginning, Castaneda did indeed undertake genuine field work as he claimed. Michael Harner, an acknowledged shaman and the editor of Castaneda's *Journey to Ixtlan*, says, "I think Castaneda's work is 110 percent valid. He conveys a deep truth, though his specific details can often be justifiably questioned."[12] Harner believes that Castaneda is simply following the traditional shamanistic practice of tricking others for their own good.

> The books of Carlos Castaneda, regardless of the questions that have been raised regarding their degree of fictionalization, have performed the valuable service of introducing many Westerners to the adventure and excitement of shamanism and to some of the legitimate principles involved.[13]

One dissertation committee member of Castaneda's, Clement Meighan, remained a solid supporter of Castaneda's throughout the years. It was an assignment in Meighan's undergraduate ethnography class that originally sent Castaneda out seeking an interview with an Indian informant. Meighan was impressed with his results from the beginning. "Obviously, he was getting information that anthropologists had not gotten before."[14] In addressing the University of California Press editorial board, he said:

I've known him since he was an undergraduate student here and I'm absolutely convinced that he is an extremely creative thinker, that he's doing anthropology. . . . He's put his finger on things that no other anthropologist has even been able to get at, partly by luck and partly because of his particular personality. He's able to get information that other anthropologists can't get, because he looks like an Indian and speaks Spanish fluently and because he's a smart listener.[15]

Respected anthropologist Mary Douglas, though admittedly concerned with processes of validation, feels that when a reader takes the lessons and goes along with the teachings, "quite a lot appears that is totally unexpected, new, and provocative."[16] She dismisses de Mille's concern that this old, uneducated Indian informant is addressing contemporary philosophical questions, and adds that these ideas are likely to promote advances in anthropology.

It may be difficult to judge the spirituality of the religion revealed in this series because of the deafening clichés in which it is perforce rendered. But it would be more difficult to defend formally the view that their echoing of contemporary philosophical concerns is proof of their bogus character. For they are consistently knitted into an attitude towards life and death and human rationality whose very coherence is alien to our own contemporary thought.[17]

Yves Marton echoes this view that Castaneda's work, aside from its possible distortion, is innovative and represents the "upper limits of what is involved in associating one's self with the spiritual world view of informants."[18] Marton bases his assessment on the similarity of descriptions of Castaneda's experiences to Marton's own. He also observes that many other anthropologists (he highlights Evans-Pritchard) recounted similar experiences that were lost in their larger work because they didn't fit within prevailing perspectives. Marton identifies the controversy surrounding Castaneda as resulting partly from "a strong bias on the part of anthropologists and academics in general against 'going native' and seriously reporting personal spiritual and/or 'supernatural' experiences" and partly from Castaneda's "process of deliberate self-mystification."[19]

Castaneda debunkers like de Mille sadly shake their heads at Douglas, Marton, and other respected researchers and thinkers whom, they believe, have been conned by Castaneda. Castaneda's methodological secrecy and his unwillingness to let others examine his field notes makes critics like de Mille smell a hoax. That same criterion, it seems, has not been applied to other, more mainstream, researchers such as Erving Goffman. Philip Manning says, "Goffman was secretive about his methods. He rarely discussed methods of data collection."[20] Goffman, he adds, felt that "honesty is best preserved by not allowing others to read [one's] field notes."[21]

Another group at the polar extreme of de Mille maintains that it makes no difference if the works of Castaneda are (using de Mille's criteria) authentic or merely valid. Joseph Margolis says, "it makes no difference whether the books are a record of an actual encounter or whether Castaneda is the author of a clever fiction."[22] Stephen Reno theorizes that given the uncertainty of a postmodern world, if don Juan did not exist, "it would be necessary to invent him."[23] He agrees with others who believe there would be no controversy if Castaneda's interesting stories were not being passed on as scientific inquiry, and adds, "For my part, I admit that after ten years, notwithstanding my rejection of its literal truth, the don Juan legend appeals to me strongly still."[24]

Marton indicates that the Castaneda controversy has caused certain research topics to be declared taboo and that certain researchers have been criticized (as Marton once was) for "sound[ing] like Castaneda." Yet Marton voices ethnography's debt to Castaneda while voicing a widespread, moderate critique of his work.[25]

Castaneda appears to have written realistic evocative ethnographic novels, introducing an innovative portrayal of participatory fieldwork, based in part on field research. The exact manner in which he obtained the data, the degree to which he accurately presented himself as he is both in and outside of his books, the precise amount of material he lived, borrowed, or invented, the actions he chose to take with his fame, and the mystique surrounding him are issues that still have not been fully resolved.[26]

Castaneda's contribution to anthropology (and his main sin) was in writing interesting, first-person narratives that appealed to a larger audience than the normal group of scholars. De Mille criticizes Castaneda for not building on the work of established mainline anthropologists such as Mircea Eliade. Yet anyone who has read Eliade's classic, *Shamanism*, can't help but admit that its dry and distant exposition gives us a dry and distant idea of shamanism that pales in comparison to the captivating and readable work of Castaneda. Marton adds:

> Examining Castaneda's work should not be taboo. . . . Many of the apparently extraordinary phenomena described in his books are reported by other competent anthropologists. In this light, Castaneda can be seen as a pioneer, if a flawed one, in synthesizing and evoking the participatory approach to encounters with a "separate reality" in anthropology.[27]

One more person has recently waded into the debate. Castaneda's first wife, Margaret Runyan Castaneda, wrote of her life with Castaneda before and during the early years of the controversy. In our day of tell-all exposés, one might expect her insider view of her elusive, self-mystifying ex-husband to end the controversy. In a way it does; in a way it doesn't. Runyan Castaneda (who, for the sake of simplicity and clarity, I will subsequently refer to simply as *Runyan*) affirms many of the views of both supporters and debunkers. She draws a biographical picture of a man who conducted legitimate research, who was changed by that research, and who wrote ethnographic novels (which included many external ideas and conversations) based on that research.

She affirms that, "all the material in Carlos' books is absolutely true."[28] She verifies the existence of don Juan and the reality of Castaneda's field experience.

> Carlos said that he was making trips into the desert to study the use of medicinal plants by Indians. "I have found a man," he told me one day; but other than saying he was an Indian and a teacher, Carlos said very little more about his excursions.[29]

And:

> The only thing for sure was that the Carlos Castaneda of the real world was making trips away from the apartment through the rest of 1960 to talk with

the Indians. He was spending less time at home. . . . For a while, he'd try to explain the importance of his trips to me, but I wasn't particularly interested. The only thing I knew was that he wasn't around the apartment very much anymore and I didn't like it. . . . I wasn't very happy with him bringing weeds into my apartment either.[30]

Runyan adds that Castaneda had even taken her son "C. J. to see his Indian friend out in the desert."[31] Absence of information does not equate to absence of its existence. Castaneda later says that don Juan's reticence to provide information about his background and personal life "was, fundamentally, a didactic device; as far as he was concerned, his time began when he became a warrior; anything that had happened to him before was of very little consequence."[32] Runyan pushes aside the anger and scorn of the debunkers and the naïveté of some supporters to affirm those who have accepted the moderate path.

Clearly, part of the conversation was fake, but "don Juan" is real. He was a real Indian, somebody Carlos actually was making trips to see. It's just that once Carlos got to the point of putting it all down in a readable form, the don Juan of his books became a different creature, a broad omniscient construction made up of equal parts of real Indian, pure Castaneda imagination, library research and dozens of conversation with people like C. J., myself, Mike Harner, colleagues at UCLA, his grandfather and others.[33]

It is possible that Carlos' [sic] first book, and presumably those that followed, was a pastiche of fact and imagination, a collection of information gleaned from the deserts of Arizona, California, and Mexico as well as the libraries of UCLA, and then assembled in a readable story form. It is also possible that the books he has written are careful and reasonably accurate records of his first years as an apprentice.[34]

Runyan also counters de Mille's lament that Castaneda refused to share his field notes with anyone and its accompanying implication that he was covering for the fact that there were no field notes. Runyan affirms the existence of actual field notes.

Carlos's years in the field had generated several hundred pages of field notes, some photographs, a brief 16mm film and some tape recorded interviews, most of which he later denied having. He reworked his field notes all along, trying to put them into a more readable form.[35]

Runyan, Harner, Marton, and others also help us understand some basic biases that lie at the source of the debunkers' displays of anger and vehemence, displays that go even beyond normal acerbic academic critique. One is the fear of descriptions of reality that differ drastically from one's own. This includes the assumption that a poor Indian informant would not be able to think the "deep" thoughts of great Western thinkers. Another is the "great fear" that Castaneda has duped everyone and, as with the "peanut butter on doorknobs crushing lice" professor from a previous chapter, supporters will eventually be exposed as fools and charlatans. Finally, Castaneda's ethnographic style of research was generally distrusted by the quantitative researchers who still fight the modernist fight in dogged pursuit of a solitary, verifiable truth.

## Cognicentrism

C. Roderick Wilson identifies *ethnocentrism* as a problem facing works like those produced by Castaneda. Alien beliefs and practices can be "respected from afar, but the moment an attempt is made to bring alien beliefs and practices into the arena of scientific investigation, one is dismissed as a crank."[36] Harner carries this beyond a conflict of cultures, saying that it is difficult to be even-handed about experiences that directly counter one's own experience of reality. He attributes this difficulty as an ingredient of the hostility facing Castaneda.

> To understand the deep-seated, emotional hostility that greeted the works of Castaneda in some quarters, one needs to keep in mind that this kind of prejudice is often involved. It is the counterpart of ethnocentrism between cultures. But in this case it is not the narrowness of someone's *cultural* experience that is the fundamental issue, but the narrowness of someone's *conscious* experience. The persons most prejudiced against a concept of nonordinary reality are those who have never experienced it. This might be termed *cognicentrism*, the analogue in consciousness of ethnocentrism.[37]

De Mille wrote, "When don Juan opens his mouth, the words of particular writers come out."[38] De Mille's implied accusation here is that Castaneda obviously fabricated some of his dialogue with don Juan. Meighan and Runyan provide an alternative view on this. Clement Meighan points out that don Juan was simply a very unique informant.

"One of the problems with don Juan," says Meighan, "and one of the reasons there is criticism of him as an informant, is that he himself is a unique individual. He is not really a member of any tribal society. . . . He's not a pure Yaqui. And, moreover, he is the type of individual who raised himself to be an intellectual. I've met other Indians like this, but they are rare. You don't find the average person who is a philosopher or thinker and concerns himself with matters except on a very superficial level."[39]

Runyan supports Meighan's view and describes a conversation between Castaneda and don Juan that would leave debunkers confused because they could not conceive of a university Ph.D. discussing philosophy with an uneducated Indian informant.

Carlos says he read a bit of Wittgenstein to don Juan one day. The old man just laughed. "Your friend Wittgenstein tied the noose too tight around the neck so he can't go anywhere."[40]

The debunkers seem hampered here by a heavy overlay of cognicentrism.

## The Great Fear

Runyan recalls the academic uproar caused by Castaneda's work and celebrity status. Academics largely believe that anything read and found interesting by the general public is innately of no academic value or validity. She calls this uproar *The Great Fear*. The fact that his work caused widespread public interest caused academics to smell a hoax. "'The Great Fear' had reared up at Haines Hall, that haunting, almost unspeakable worry that maybe the whole thing was some kind of elaborate hoax."[41] Clement Meighan, Castaneda's ardent supporter, defended his student to the UCLA editorial board. "The sorts of things he is coming in with are too damned good. Even to fake it, you'd have to study anthropology for ten years in order to provide the kind of convincers or data he comes up with."[42]

Academic envy was also at work here. Runyan perceives that those who feared Castaneda were not jealous, so much as envious of this popular, young upstart who hadn't yet paid his dues and who had forsaken a lifetime of toiling in obscurity for instant popularity.

It wasn't that the detractors in the department were jealous of Carlos or anything, but more than one of them had considered their own scholarly lives, of hopsack and musty libraries and respectable gray anonymity. They knew the paperwork and the bureaucracy and all the bullshit you had to go through, the endless political jockeying for position. And they'd heard all about Carlos' [sic] teaching experience at Irvine and how the classroom was jammed all the time with people squatting everywhere. . . . Given that alternative, who *wouldn't* want that? Who among them, hadn't dreamt of crossing the line into that forbidden territory, where they talk about you at the New York cocktail parties and they silk-screen your words on posters that land in the rustic little Pacific Coast cottages in British Columbia.[43]

## Quantitative Research Paradigm

Runyan points out that the statistical, quantitative research paradigm that prevailed in the late 1950s social sciences attempted to make social research respectable by adapting the research techniques of the natural sciences to the social sciences. Readers may remember the chapter 2 discussion on the modernist perspective that fuels this type of thinking.

Social sciences would never achieve the precision of chemistry or physics, but with the increasing use of testing and statistical analysis, they were approaching what some scholars felt to be reality. The idea was to get into the little black box of the brain and the tool had become numbers and chi-square analysis.[44]

Ethnography was not completely out of favor, but what exacerbated the Castaneda problem was his elimination of any pretense of objectivity about the experiences he was undergoing. Instead of standing apart from his experiences, he was literally immersed in them and used the persona of Carlos as a foil for the maneuvers of don Juan.

What really irritated this group was the rejection of the standard procedure of being a detached observer without ego, and they didn't like it that Castaneda was carrying it off so well. Suddenly, Carlos Castaneda was the most famous anthropologist in America, but the boys back in the department had let go with a swelling academic chorus that rose up out of the faculty lounge at Haines Hall like the fulsome cry of a pair of jackals—

where was the objectivity, where was the detachment, where was the chi-square analysis?[45]

Finally, Castaneda elicited the ultimate outrage with his violation of the sacred prohibition against "going native."

Part of the controversy surrounding Castaneda results from a strong bias on the part of anthropologists and academics in general against "going native" and seriously reporting personal spiritual and/or "supernatural" experiences.[46]

Ethnographers constantly remind themselves—lest they be reminded by their colleagues—never to "go native," never to become one of "them," lest the resulting ethnography become a naïve espousal of another people's world view and ethos thus losing all objective and scientific value. The challenger is "to be one with them yet not one of them."[47]

Castaneda's flagrant violation of this prohibition outraged research purists who were attempting to raise the status of the social sciences. It also offended their cognicentrist abhorrence of scientific affirmation of a native reality. In this view, Castaneda was proposing as reality that which simply could not be real.

Runyan offers a helpful view of Castaneda's work that helps to summarize the debate over whether or not Castaneda's work is valid.

It's all there, and in the beginning Carlos Castaneda was rather careful to get it down accurately. Of course, he'd always interjected a lot of himself into his books, and the truth is, they were never pure anthropology and were never supposed to be. After all, hadn't Walter Goldschmidt, the resident god at UCLA, described *The Teachings* as both ethnography and allegory in his flowing foreword to the book? Hadn't the old man come right out and said . . . allegory . . . as if to say Carlos was blending certain levels here.

So it wasn't like it was a secret or anything, that some of the material in Carlos's books was absolutely real world fact, while some was, admittedly, a bit more subjective. What Carlos had been doing from the beginning was weaving these little stories, these aperçus, the real desert experiences and dreams, the honest dialogue of a dozen informants—weaving all this together with the details of his rather mundane Los Angeles lifestyle.[48]

Castaneda himself seems to affirm this viewpoint and to combine it
with Harner's comments on the problem of cognicentrism in the introduction to one of his books.

> Although I am an anthropologist, this is not strictly an anthropological
> work; yet it has its roots in cultural anthropology, for it began years ago as
> field research in that discipline. . . . I am very far away from my point of
> origin as an average Western man or as an anthropologist, and I must first
> of all reiterate that this is not a work of fiction. What I am describing is alien
> to us; therefore, it seems unreal.[49]

Castaneda also responds to his critics through the words of don Juan in
the popular press version of his dissertation.

> I have to tell you that it really doesn't matter whether or not all this is true.
> It is here that a warrior has a point of advantage over the average man. An
> average man cares that things are either true or false, but a warrior doesn't.
> An average man proceeds in a specific way with things that he knows are
> true, and in a different way with things that he knows are not true. If things
> are said to be true, he acts and believes in what he does. A warrior, on the
> other hand, acts in both instances.[50]

## WHAT TO DO WITH CASTANEDA

In the end, the purpose of this discussion is to let the reader know that
Castaneda was a controversial figure and that the authenticity of his work
is suspect. It is also to highlight an important point covered earlier. We
live in a constructed world where capital T "Truth" is elusive. The essential debunker argument is that Castaneda didn't conduct the field work he
describes; yet, the debunker argument is flawed by its own baggage and
its own set of cognicentric blinders. Meighan and Runyan Castaneda verify that Carlos Castaneda did indeed do field work (at least at the beginning), and fellow shamanic explorers Harner and Marton authenticate
Castaneda's experiential descriptions. The slippery verdict seems to be
that Castaneda worked from real experience and enhanced his popularized
version of it with fictionalized elements, a type of television movie "based
on real events." The ratio of fact to fiction is subject to dispute.

As a nonanthropologist, it is not my intention to authenticate Castaneda's work, but I personally tend to resonate with the arguments of the moderates. I approach Castaneda's work as valid and at least partially authentic, and I find his writings intriguing and thought provoking. At worst, he wrote a totally fictional story, a myth, highlighting the authentic findings of others; even if I believed it to simply be a work of fiction, I would use it still. Something need not be scientifically authentic to contain truth; great stories often contain a validity missed by scientific accounts. I intend to utilize Castaneda's truths whether they are authentic science or simply true myths.

> Myths are stories told by traditional religious peoples to make sense of their existence, sacred narratives recounting events in the past that give clues to life in the present. . . . Myths are true—not as history is true when substantiated by evidence—but as any story is true that fits the expectations and understandings of the listener.[51]

Castaneda's work offers us much to consider. However, we are going to look at his work primarily from a perspective of teaching and learning. Of primary focus will be the methods don Juan employs in taking this pathetic apprentice, Carlos, and helping him transform into a sorcerer. Fact or myth, this is a valuable story.

## DON JUAN'S SORCERY

### Shaman or Sorcerer

Both Lévi-Strauss and Castaneda initially use the term *sorcerer* to describe the individuals with whom they interact, but both make it clear that the term carries inaccurate baggage in our contemporary society. Lévi-Strauss changes terms in mid-narrative, stating that the term *shaman* might be better used in place of *sorcerer* as it is "a better term for their specific type of activity in certain regions of the world."[52] However, while acknowledging that *sorcerer* provides an inaccurate and limiting definition of his teacher, don Juan, Castaneda continues to use it throughout his works because language seems to lack a more exact and appropriate term.

It is important, given the emotional connotations attached to the words, to first consider the questions: what is a *sorcerer* and what is *sorcery*? In his first book, Castaneda calls don Juan a *brujo*, essentially a practitioner of dark magic. By his third book, *Journey to Ixtlan*, he settles into calling him a *sorcerer*. Even in his last books, where he begins to sprinkle in the word *shaman*, he wrestles with the inadequacy of any term to describe don Juan or his teachings. His developing understanding of the nature of sorcery is reflected with representative quotations from his early, middle, and later writings.

> I have maintained the practice of referring to that system as sorcery and I have also maintained the practice of referring to don Juan as a sorcerer, because these are categories he himself used.[53]

> because [don Juan] was unable to find a more appropriate name, he called it "sorcery," although he admitted it was not really accurate. . . . Over the years, he had given me different definitions of sorcery, but he always maintained that definitions change as knowledge increases.[54]

> "To be a sorcerer," don Juan continued, "doesn't mean to practice witchcraft, or to work to affect people, or to be possessed by demons. To be a sorcerer means to reach a level of awareness that makes inconceivable things available. The term 'sorcery' is inadequate to express what sorcerers do, and so is the term 'shamanism.'"[55]

> he taught me sorcery, but not as we understand sorcery in the context of our daily world: the use of supernatural powers over others, or the calling of spirits through charms, spells, or rituals to produce supernatural effects. For don Juan, sorcery was the act of embodying some specialized theoretical and practical premises about the nature and role of perception in molding the universe around us. . . . I realized that calling it sorcery obscures even more the already obscure phenomena he presented to me in his teachings.[56]

It is Castaneda's shaman friend, Michael Harner, who provides insight into don Juan's use of the word *sorcerer* rather than *shaman*. He suggests that *shaman* is a generic term and *sorcerer* a more specific subset of it.

> One of the things I should note . . . is that Castaneda does not emphasize healing in his books, although this is generally one of the most important

tasks of shamanism. Perhaps this is because his don Juan is basically engaged in the warrior (or sorcerer) type of shamanism.[57]

An important role of the shaman involves healing and the restoration of physical and spiritual balance to both individuals and communities. We see none of this in the Castaneda books, in which the role of the sorcerer is to see beyond the constructs of a culture and to work directly with an admittedly incomprehensible universe. Using Harner's distinction, I intend to refer to Castaneda's specific contribution to shamanism as *sorcery* while referring more generically to others' contributions as *shamanism*.

## The Shaman and the Sacred

Eliade helps connect the idea of shamanism to Durkheim's perception of the roles of the sacred and the profane in society. If the sacred is the glue that holds society together, intimates of sacred matters hold a special role and are responsible for preserving and defending the sacred amidst the profane aspect of ordinary existence. For Mircea Eliade, the shaman "can be defined as a specialist in the sacred, that is, an individual who participates in the sacred more completely, or more truly, than other men."[58]

Castaneda's warrior–sorcerer defines *sorcery* in terms of distinguishing between the sacred (sorcery) and the profane (ordinary). A warrior is taught to perceive sacred warrior aspects of reality unavailable to ordinary profane perception.

that is sorcery: the ability to use energy fields that are not employed in perceiving the ordinary world we know. Sorcery is a state of awareness. Sorcery is the ability to perceive something which ordinary perception cannot.[59]

Warriors change their views of the world by learning to *see* things differently than an ordinary person. Don Juan says, "Seeing, of course, is the final accomplishment of a man of knowledge."[60]

According to Castaneda's don Juan, only two possibilities exist for us in life. "We choose either to be warriors or to be ordinary men. A second choice does not exist."[61] Throughout the Castaneda volumes, the notion of being a warrior distills down to the principle of total responsibility for every aspect of one's life. This is not a contemporary, meticulously qualified version of responsibility. Don Juan spells this out succinctly when he says, "The basic difference between an ordinary man and a warrior is that a warrior takes everything as a challenge . . . while an ordinary man takes everything either as a blessing or a curse."[62]

For Castaneda, sorcery has a constructivist, postmodern quality to it. Don Juan teaches Carlos that the reality to which he clings is simply a construction; he initially utilizes psychotropic drugs to prod Carlos to recognize this fact. Even the sorcerers' reality, he says, is just another construction. Reality lies between the constructions, and a warrior who lives an impeccable life is able to take advantage of that space between realities.

> "The first truth is that the world is as it looks and yet it isn't," he went on. "It's not as solid and real as our perception has been led to believe, but it isn't a mirage either. The world is not an illusion, as it has been said to be; it's real on the one hand, and unreal on the other. Pay close attention to this, for it must be understood, not just accepted. We perceive. This is a hard fact. But what we perceive is not a fact of the same kind, because we learn what to perceive. . . . Something out there is affecting our senses. This is the part that is real. The unreal part is what our senses tell us is there."[63]

Researchers indicate that all shamans are not equal. Some shamans have a greater affinity for the vocation and are able to forge a stronger connection to the sacred than others. According to Harner, "only a few shamans become true masters of knowledge, power, and healing."[64] Eliade explains that it isn't enough to simply "want" to be a shaman.

> Religious experience and knowledge have degrees, higher and yet higher planes, which, by their very nature cannot be attained by all. Deeper religious experience and knowledge require a special vocation, or exceptional willpower and intelligence. Just as a man cannot become a shaman or a mystic simply by wanting to, so he cannot rise to certain initiatory degrees unless he demonstrates that he possesses spiritual qualities.[65]

Castaneda's don Juan describes this point in his typically colorful manner.

> there are scores of imbeciles who become seers. Seers are human beings full of foibles, or rather, human beings full of foibles are capable of becoming seers. Just as in the case of miserable people who become superb

scientists. . . . The characteristic of miserable seers is that they are willing to forget the wonder of the world. They become overwhelmed by the fact that they see and believe it is their genius that counts. . . . More important than seeing itself is what seers do with what they see.[66]

Don Juan employs a particular term for a warrior who has reached the pinnacle of sorcery. He calls such a person, a *man of knowledge*. While this chauvinistic term is inappropriate in our time and culture, we need to remember that both don Juan's cultural paradigm and the bulk of Castaneda's writing about that paradigm predate feminist insights. We need to recognize as well that Castaneda's writing is filled with powerful, accomplished female sorcerers.

"A man of knowledge is one who has followed truthfully the hardships of learning," he said. "A man who has, without rushing or without faltering, gone as far as he can in unraveling the secrets of power and knowledge."
"Can anyone be a man of knowledge?"
"No, not anyone."[67]

## SHAMANIC LEARNING AND SILENT KNOWLEDGE

Shamanism is ultimately about learning. Harner said, "Shamanism is, after all, basically a strategy for personal learning and acting on that learning."[68] There is no shortcut to becoming a shaman. It takes work; it takes experience; it takes time. Harner states, "shamanic initiation is experiential and often gradual."[69] Both Eliade and Castaneda agree that two types of instruction are necessary. An apprentice must master the profane knowledge attached to the practice of shamanism and must experience the sacred knowledge that comes only through direct experience with the sacred.

a shaman is recognized as such only after having received two kinds of instruction. The first is ecstatic (e.g., dreams, visions, trances); the second is traditional (e.g., shamanic techniques, names and functions of the spirits, mythology and genealogy of the clan, secret language). This twofold teaching, imparted by the spirits and the old master shamans, constitutes initiation.[70]

Sorcerers, therefore, divided their instruction into two categories. One was the instruction for the everyday-life. . . . The other was instruction for the states of heightened awareness . . . without the distracting intervention of spoken language.[71]

To facilitate the two different types of instruction, a certain sleight of hand is employed. Because we humans tend to protect our world views and resist real learning, shamans use the traditional teachings (techniques, names, mythologies) and the ecstatic experiences to conceal the fact that they are sending apprentices down a path of significant transformation. Once the concealed teachings are internalized, apprentices can no longer look at the profane world as they once had. Castaneda, in his commentary for the thirtieth anniversary edition of *Teachings*, said a genuine internalization of such rationales entails a transformation, a different response to the world of everyday life. Shamans found out that the initial thrust of this transformation always occurs as an intellectual allegiance to something that appears to be merely a concept, but that has unsuspected powerful undercurrents.[72]

Everything is simply a device intended to convince an apprentice that the sacred intersects with the profane in endless ways, "that there's more to us than meets the eye."[73] Although an apprentice might feel he is learning sorcery, says don Juan, "all he's doing is allowing himself to be convinced of the power in his being."[74] Don Juan utilizes an insightful term for this sleight-of-hand learning. He calls it *silent knowledge*. "You will need a lifetime to remember the insights you've had today," he said, "because most of them were silent knowledge."[75] It seems the really important things we learn are often not discrete and explicit enough even to be consciously recognized because the learned elements cannot be extracted from their context.

Guédon points out the transformative nature of such learning, describing how material tasks elicited deeper personal transformation. She explains that she was taught not to embroider moccasins but to become a moccasin embroiderer, not to hunt but to become a hunter.[76] She echoes Castaneda's assertion that traditional teachings are conceptualized in a way that includes powerful undercurrents.

Learning is also always conceptualized. One learns the place and time where knowledge can be put into action, and the information is never divorced from its application and its natural and social environment. Furthermore, information is not divided into bits to be assembled later but is kept together as aspects of a whole process. Finally, the information itself . . . does not matter as much as the relationship process it sets in motion between the learner, the teacher, and the environment.[77]

## THE SHAMAN'S STRATEGY

Throughout Castaneda's writings, don Juan reveals the strategies he used to overcome Castaneda's instinctual resistance to the destruction and transformation of his established world view. Key elements of these cumulative strategies comprise the Shaman's Strategy (see figure 4.1).

### Hooking and Misdirection

The first step in apprentice education is the process of "hooking" apprentices and misleading them into thinking they will be studying something they *want* to study. Don Juan tells Carlos that he "hooked" him with his warrior's gaze, adding that this is only a way of describing something that in fact defies description. Don Juan encouraged Carlos to believe he would be gaining esoteric knowledge about psychotropic plants, while actually having very different plans for him.

> "Once the apprentice has been hooked, the instruction begins," he continued. "The first act of a teacher is to introduce the idea that the world we think we see is only a view, a description of the world. Every effort of a teacher is geared to prove this point to his apprentice. But accepting it seems to be one of the hardest things one can do; we are complacently caught in our particular view of the world, which compels us to feel and act as if we knew everything about the world. A teacher from the very first act he performs aims at stopping that view."[78]

---

1. Apprentice is "hooked" and misdirected.
2. Apprentice is tricked into world view reconstruction.
3. Body attention is redirected through ritual and acting "as if" one were already professional.
4. Cognitive attention is redirected through myth.
5. Apprentice experiences loss and decides whether or not to continue.

---

**Figure 4.1    The Shaman's Strategy**

Shamans hook apprentices to secure their willingness to accept instruction. As apprentices are innately reluctant to abandon familiar world views, shamans hook apprentices with promises to teach them the things they actually want to learn. It isn't that the hook is a total deception; it is more that the hook occupies a tangential role in the total world view that is to be transmitted. Castenada, for example, did indeed learn about psychotropic plants, but in his introduction to *Ixtlan*, he reports that this primary objective faded into the background as his view of the world changed.

Professional education unconsciously utilizes a similar hooking approach. Students come to professional education for a variety of reasons that are typically tangential to the actual work of the profession. Younger students are often attracted by some smaller task that they project onto the broader profession. Education students often "like children" and computer students often "like graphic design." These are good starting points, as prospective teachers ought to like children and prospective computer professionals ought to be interested in graphic design, but these interests fail to capture the essential work of the profession. Older students returning to school after working in other occupations are often lured by the promise of steady or lucrative employment. For these students, these are the hooks that have almost nothing to do with the work of the profession. Yet all of these students are, in a sense, hooked.

Once hooked, the world view dismantling process begins immediately. After hooking Carlos, don Juan immediately works to erode his confidence in his "ordinary" world view and replace it with a "warrior" world view.

> in the case of my apprenticeship, don Juan was not concerned at all with whether or not I could take his proposition seriously, and he proceeded to elucidate his points, in spite of my opposition, my disbelief, and my ability to understand what he was saying. Thus, as a teacher of sorcery, don Juan endeavored to describe the world to me from the very first time we talked.[79]

To accomplish this, don Juan puts him through a series of experiences calculated to weaken the foundations of what he considered reality. The first step in this process is to introduce the idea that the "real" world isn't as "real" as it first appears. By weakening that description, don Juan was able to insert another description in its place. Kalweit affirms the universality of this practice in shamanic apprenticeships.

All shamanic experiences of initiation involve a deautomization of ordinary consciousness. A shamanic technique may be anything that disrupts and confuses the normal stream of thoughts, the habitual experience of emotions and ordinary physiological processes, and then produces a new rhythmic pattern. Such techniques are universally employed by all esoteric and spiritual schools, secret societies, orders of healers, and so on.[80]

Research indicates that our world perceptions arise from habitual structures that can quickly be disrupted or destroyed by biochemical or neurological changes. "It takes surprisingly little to turn human consciousness upside down or cause it to disintegrate."[81]

Don Juan initially works with Carlos to get him to "stop the world." For don Juan this term implied a total break with the certainty of the ordinary view of reality. This break is accomplished by pitting ordinary reality against a warrior's reality. The Castaneda books are filled with explanations, descriptions, and narratives of how warriors (in contrast to ordinary people) conduct their lives. Don Juan describes to Carlos the inner terrain of a warrior's world.

the secret of a warrior is that he believes without believing. . . . A warrior, whenever he has to involve himself with believing, does it as a choice, as an expression of his innermost predilection. A warrior doesn't believe, a warrior has to believe.[82]

"A rule of thumb for a warrior," he said, "is that he makes his decisions so carefully that nothing that may happen as a result of them can surprise him, much less drain his power."[83]

Yet most of don Juan's teachings were not so overt. In fact, we learn the most about don Juan's techniques in retrospect, when he reveals them to Carlos after they have already served their purpose and after Carlos has had many years to recognize them and reflect upon them. In one of his last books, Castaneda says, "That was don Juan's style of teaching. He veiled the importance of several maneuvers behind the mundane."[84]

Many of the same techniques are unconsciously applied when professional students are effectively educated. Students who have been hooked into a professional program are immediately enjoined to begin looking at the world through the eyes of that profession. Even in mixed introductory classes, professional majors are given special attention and are nudged in the direction of professional thought and behavior. Students who do not seem amenable to this nudging are quickly marked by professional faculty as not being prime professional candidates. Those who do seem adaptable and who advance past introductory courses undergo a more concentrated assault on their "ordinary" world view and are given more detailed instruction as to the proper way to conduct themselves. Adherence to this "professional" world view becomes an imperative.

## Trickery and World View Reconstruction: Everyday Knowledge, Silent Knowledge, and Pseudotasks

The apprentice's education includes a great deal of attention to practical, everyday information important to a shaman. Castenada, for example, is taught about psychotropic plants and is taught all of the overt information necessary for him to lead the visible life of a warrior. Intertwined with this everyday knowledge is the covert knowledge invisible to everyone except the teacher. The everyday knowledge, although important in its own right, conceals the more important world view knowledge that would be resisted if presented directly.

### Pseudotasks

> He laughed and said that his maneuver had been so subtle that it had bypassed me to that day. Then he reminded me of all the nonsensical joking tasks that he used to give me every time I had been at his house. Absurd chores such as arranging firewood in patterns, encircling his house with an unbroken chain of concentric circles drawn in the dirt with my finger, sweeping debris from one place to another, and so forth. The tasks also included acts that I had to perform by myself at home, such as wearing a black cap, or tying my left shoe first, or fastening my belt from right to left.
>
> Carlos Castaneda, *Tales of Power* (New York: Pocket Books, 1976), 237.

Don Juan asserts that this concentrated assault on a world view necessarily involves tricking an apprentice. He tells Carlos, "Sorcerers are convinced that all of us are a bunch of nincompoops . . . we can never relinquish our crummy control voluntarily, thus we have to be tricked."[85] To trick Carlos, don Juan uses pseudotasks: tasks intended to get Carlos to think the task was the focus of attention while the silent, world view change that was taking place had time to establish itself. This strategy was designed to direct Carlos's attention without encountering the direct, protective resistance it would have encountered if the attempt to alter his world view had been evident.

> A teacher must not leave anything to chance. I've told you that you were correct in feeling that you were being tricked. The problem was that you were convinced that that tricking was directed at fooling your reason. For me, tricking meant to distract your attention, or to trap it as the case required.[86]

An abundance of pseudotasks likewise await fledgling professional students. The aspects of their learning that they initially feel are so important often are pseudotasks that quickly fade into the background of professional practice. To an extent, this is a continuation of the "hooking" process that brought them into the program. Through these pseudotasks, students are convinced of the importance of activities such as attending lectures and reading textbooks and completing assignments, even as those very activities divert their attention from the fundamental world view changes that are taking place internally.

## Body Attention and Ritual

It is here that Durkheim's concept of ritual and myth as vehicles for transmitting culture join with don Juan's concept of silent knowledge. Don Juan regularly makes the point to Castenada that most of his learning is between the lines and unconscious. Durkheim makes similar claims. It is important to remember that Durkheimian ritual is more encompassing than formal theatrical ceremonies, and Durkheimian myth is more encompassing than stories about Greek and Roman gods. Randall Collins clarifies the role that Durkheim assigned to ritual in the development and transference of cultural ideas and practices. "For Durkheim, a ritual is a particular kind of configuration of human beings focusing their bodies, attentions, and emotions in a certain way."[87] This clarification highlights the similarities between this idea espoused by Durkheim and the many espoused by don Juan. Both focus on the body and the importance of attention. "When one does something with people," don Juan said, "the concern should be only with presenting the case to their bodies. That's what I've been doing with you so far, letting your body know. Who cares whether or not you understand?"[88]

Bruce Lincoln offers an important insight concerning Durkheim's representation of ritual and myth. He says that although ritual and myth intertwine and overlap, ritual is primarily "gestural and dramatic," and myth is primarily "verbal and narrative."[89] This allows us to define *ritual* in terms of action and *myth* in terms of narrative. Durkheim and Goffman both viewed the emotion and focused attention of ritual as a means of transmitting important cultural ideas. Kalweit draws upon this view when he redefines the concept of ceremonies.

We should stop thinking of ceremonies as fixed rituals that consist of meaningless and empty repetitions of verbal formulae, along with rigidly patterned gestures. . . . The attention, so diffused in normal states, focuses on a single point, the needle's eye of consciousness. Pushing it, drumming it, singing it through that hole into another dimension in which space and time, the fundamental categories of human experience of the world possess a different quality—that is the work of the ceremony.[90]

Rituals also encompass several other important aspects of apprenticeship. Through rituals, an apprentice learns the secret esoteric language, learns the powerful cultural symbols, and learns appropriate behavior from nonverbal language of others. A previous chapter notes the power of language in shaping our reality. Kalweit points out that the sacred language brings shaman apprentices in contact with higher powers and provides them with a way of conversing with each other in a way not understood by other members of the tribe.[91] Kalweit also notes that rituals work through the use of symbols that clarify the "polarities, forces and relationships of existence" and provide a most effective means for humans to express the abstract forces of nature.[92] Guédon notes that the simplest rituals provide subtle instruction in the intricacies of the culture. She notes that, "I noticed how the old women, especially, would look at me, and with a glance, stop me from making the wrong move; and reward me similarly for the right gesture."[93]

Schools offer endless opportunities for rituals that quietly provide cultural information for students and help them define their place within a culture. Many of the rituals might not be recognized as such by individuals who think of ritual on a grander scale. Peter McLaren makes this clear when he says, "Even the words on this page, which have been chosen to develop the themes and ideas for this research, are themselves part of a ritual event"; he goes on to quote Ronald L. Grimes, who said, "Pen and paper are power objects, fetishes; theorizing and observing are ritual gestures laden with ideology."[94] If we use the definition of ritual as something that focuses a body's attention in specific directions, we see that ritual abounds. Students participate in ritual by attending classes, doing assignments, working on joint projects, taking exams, and talking with teachers and other students. All of these encounters pass along explicit and implicit information about the totality of what is expected by someone who has mastered this profession.

A key item that separates a warrior from an ordinary person is that a warrior *acts like* a warrior long before he or she actually becomes one. Acquisition of a new world view is a process, not a discrete event. If an aspiring warrior were to continue to act like an ordinary person and wait for warriorhood to arrive, it would never happen. In a sense, a warrior is claiming what is already on the inside rather than expecting it to arrive from the outside. It is the acting as if one were already a warrior that helps facilitate the world view change of becoming one.

> [Don Juan] whispered that a warrior acted as if he knew what he was doing, when in effect he knew nothing. . . . He said, "A warrior is impeccable when he trusts his personal power regardless of whether it is small or enormous."[95]

Throughout the apprenticeship, apprentices must act as if they know what they are doing even though they do not. Not only must the student act this way, so must the teacher. The teacher knows that, by undergoing the traditional ritualistic and mythical teaching, a student is likely to transform into a shaman. Neither the teacher nor the student knows *how* this happens. Not unlike quantum physicists, shamans know that certain things will work as they do, but they don't really understand why they work. Don Juan says, "the extraordinary thing is that the performer has no way of knowing how these things happen. In other words, Genaro doesn't know how he does those things; he only knows that he does them."[96] Even shamans must act as if they know why something works, yet don Juan freely admits on several occasions that although he and don Genaro know that something *will* work, they don't know *why* it works.

## Cognitive Attention and Myth

Culture is also transmitted through narrative accounts. According to Durkheim, a group's mythology is a "system of beliefs common to this group. The traditions whose memory it perpetuates express the way in which society represents man and the world; it is a moral system and a cosmology as well as a history."[97] Eliade calls the mythology of a culture its "sacred history" and describes it as the "foundation for all human behavior and all social and cultural institutions."[98]

Artificial intelligence expert Roger Schank might describe myths simply as stories that simultaneously create and are molded by our perceptions of reality:

> People think in terms of stories. They understand the world in terms of stories that they have already understood. New events or problems are understood by reference to old previously understood stories and explained to others by the use of stories. We understand personal problems and relationships between people through stories that typify those situations. We also understand just about everything else this way as well. Scientists have prototypical scientific success and failure stories that they use to help them with new problems. Historians have their favorite stories in terms of which they understand and explain the world. Stories are very basic to the human thinking process.[99]

Schank accurately notes that such stories need not be epic in nature. The stories we tell each other illustrate our views of the world, and the stories told within professions define and enforce professional boundaries and expectations, indirectly and effectively.

Schools offer professional students ample opportunity to hear and tell stories. Stories told by teachers and "upper division" students provide a great deal of information to younger apprentices as to how they should view their professional worlds. Again, these need not be formal presentations. They may be stray comments laden with information. I still re-member a comment I heard from a lab assistant on my first foray into the scary turf of my first computer lab. The young woman looked up at me as I timidly checked in and said simply, "This is *not* a happy place." The fact that this simple statement captured the essence of my experience in that lab might account for the fact that I have never forgotten it. It formed one of the first bricks in my computer lab mythology.

## Loss and Decision

> "Your world is coming to an end," he said. "It is the end of an era for you. Do you think that the world you have known all your life is going to leave you peacefully, without any fuss or muss? No! It will wiggle underneath you, and hit you with its tail."
>
> Carlos Castaneda, *Active Side of Infinity* (New York: Harper Perennial, 2000), 87.

The rite of passage into a shaman's world typically involves a metaphor of death and rebirth, implying an erasing of one's former world view and an entry into a new one.[100] The path to facilitate this change in-volves suffering, which causes "the disintegration of one's own system of thought in order to perceive a new world in the higher space."[101] Be-cause an apprentice is asked to leave behind a life to assume a new one, the teacher eventually requires that the apprentice make a conscious de-cision to continue on the path even though the outcome of that decision is typically preordained by the nature and training of the apprentice.

In his book *Journey to Ixtlan*, Castaneda dramatically illustrates the dev-astating loss involved. In it, don Juan describes the loss incurred by fellow shaman don Genaro in a passage that gives meaning to the title of the book:

> What Genaro told you in his story is precisely that Genaro left his passion in Ixtlan: his home, his people, all the things he cared for. And now he wan-ders around in his feelings; and sometimes, as he says, he almost reaches Ixtlan.[102]

The completeness and permanence of such a loss requires that the shaman issue a warning at a key point and that an apprentice make a decision whether

or not to continue. The choice involves whether to continue on the sacred
path of the warrior or the profane path of ordinary people.

> The apprentice must choose between the warrior's world and his ordinary
> world. But no decision is possible unless the apprentice understands the
> choice; thus a teacher must have a thoroughly patient and understanding at-
> titude and must lead his man with a sure hand to that choice and above all
> he must make sure that his apprentice chooses the world and the life of a
> warrior.[103]

Castaneda writes, "In other words, the belief system I wanted to study
swallowed me, and in order for me to proceed with my scrutiny I have to
make an extraordinary daily payment, my life as a man in this world."[104]
The price of choosing the warrior's path is that one will never again be
able to return to life on the ordinary path.

Yet a formal choice is not the same thing as a conscious choice. The decision comes from somewhere beyond our conscious understanding; it is
something we cannot understand, something that we can only acknowledge. We only think we decide. According to don Juan: "When we think
we decide, all we're doing is acknowledging that something beyond our
understanding has set up the frame of our so-called decision, and all we
do is to acquiesce."[105]

This decision is only presented after an apprentice has undertaken a
requisite amount of suffering, because suffering shakes the foundation of
established realities and permits the uncertainty of new ones. It is a goal
of shamanic teaching. The idea of learning through suffering is a difficult
one for our culture. Kalweit, after describing it as an essential element of
shamanic learning, discusses this difficulty for our culture.

> No civilized person believes in finding salvation through pain. Rendered se-
> cure by the existence of hospitals and the medical establishment, Western-
> ers banishes [*sic*] all suffering from their perspective. Since it has required
> all our effort and intelligence to keep suffering out of our world, why should
> we bring it back in again?[106]

In our culture, we try to protect our students not only from suffering
but also from any type of discomfort whatsoever. It is assumed that students ought not to "suffer" any sort of discomfort as they move through

the educational process. The closest resemblance to suffering in contemporary education is the angst caused by assignments and exams. As a tragic result, students are generally spared the transformation that results from discomfort and suffering. This ban on suffering makes our education palatable but ineffective, as it eliminates a major tool involved in dissolving an old world view.

## CONCLUSION

The end of the apprenticeship process means that the new shaman now sees the world differently without knowing how the transition occurred. Kalweit quoted shaman Knud Rasmussen as saying, "I became a shaman, not knowing myself how it came about. But I was a shaman. I could see and hear in a totally different way."[107] This echoes the description of real learning promoted by Donald Schön. Real learning by definition involves transformation that causes one to see things differently. Castaneda describes this as gaining membership.

The termination of the apprenticeship meant that I had learned a new description of the world in a convincing and authentic manner and thus I had become capable of eliciting a new perception of the world, which matched its new description. In other words, I had gained membership.[108]

One last question remains to conclude a shaman's training. What happens once an apprentice has achieved membership in this new world view? The answer is that the new world view needs to permeate the apprentice and fuse with the individual's unique temperament to give a distinctive twist to both profane and sacred acts.

"Once we have reached it, what exactly do we do with it, don Juan?"
"Nothing. Once we have reached it, it will, by itself, make use of energy fields that are available to us but inaccessible. . . . And what any of us does with that increased perception, with that silent knowledge, depends on our own temperament."[109]

The end of the formal apprenticeship is the beginning of a unique encounter with the world. The new shaman needs to spend much time discovering and recognizing the lessons embedded in the silent knowledge learned in the apprenticeship and needs to learn how to utilize the new vision that has been created through it.

The Shaman's Strategy described in this chapter closed the circle for me that began with the questions I asked in the first chapter. It seemed to describe the process that worked for me and the process that worked (and didn't work) for my students. I undertook the following case study to see how well it worked under the microscope of formal observation.

## NOTES

1. Michael Harner, *The Way of the Shaman* (New York: Harper & Row, 1990), 20.

2. Walter Goldschmidt, foreword to *The Teachings of Don Juan: A Yaqui Way of Knowledge,* by Carlos Castaneda (New York: Ballantine Books, 1968), viii.

3. Richard de Mille, "The Shaman of Academe," in *The Don Juan Papers: Further Castaneda Controversies*, ed. Richard de Mille (Belmont, Calif.: Wadsworth Publishing, 1990), 18–20.

4. Richard de Mille, "Validity Is Not Authenticity," in *The Don Juan Papers: Further Castaneda Controversies*, ed. Richard de Mille (Belmont, Calif.: Wadsworth Publishing, 1990).

5. Sanford Berman, "Cataloging Castaneda," in *The Don Juan Papers: Further Castaneda Controversies*, ed. Richard de Mille (Belmont, Calif.: Wadsworth Publishing, 1990), 100.

6. Stephen O. Murray, "The Invisibility of Scientific Scorn," in *The Don Juan Papers: Further Castaneda Controversies*, ed. Richard de Mille (Belmont, Calif.: Wadsworth Publishing, 1990), 201.

7. Hans Sebald, "Roasting Rabbits in Tularemia or the Lion, the Witch, and the Horned Toad," in *The Don Juan Papers: Further Castaneda Controversies*, ed. Richard de Mille (Belmont, Calif.: Wadsworth Publishing, 1990), 38.

8. Richard McDermott, "Reasons, Rules, and the Ring of Experience: Reading Our World into Carlos Castaneda's Works," *Human Studies* 2, no. 1, (January 1979): 31–46.

9. Paul Riesman, "Fictions of Art and Science, or Does It Matter whether Don Juan Really Exists?" in *The Don Juan Papers: Further Castaneda Controversies*, ed. Richard de Mille (Belmont, Calif.: Wadsworth Publishing, 1990), 207.

10. Reisman, "Fictions," 209.

11. Reisman, "Fictions," 215–216.

12. Quoted in de Mille, "Shaman," 22.

13. Harner, *Shaman*, xxiii.

14. Quoted in Margaret Runyan Castaneda, *A Magical Journey with Carlos Castaneda* (Victoria, Canada: Millennia Press, 1997), 84.

15. Quoted in Runyan Castaneda, *Magical Journey*, 123–124.

16. Mary Douglas, "The Authenticity of Castaneda," in *Implicit Meanings: Essays in Anthropology*, ed. Mary Douglas (London: Routledge, 1993), 197.

17. Douglas, "Castaneda," 199.

18. Yves Marton, "The Experiential Approach to Anthropology and Castaneda's Ambiguous Legacy," in *Being Changed: The Anthropology of Extraordinary Experience*, ed. David. E. Young and Jean-Guy Goulet (Ontario, Canada: Broadview Press, 1994), 274.

19. Marton, "Castaneda's Legacy," 281.

20. Philip Manning, *Erving Goffman and Modern Sociology* (Stanford, Calif.: Stanford University Press, 1992), 142.

21. Manning, *Goffman*, 154.

22. Quoted in de Mille, "Validity Is Not Authenticity," 39.

23. Stephen J. Reno, "If Don Juan Did Not Exist, It Would Be Necessary to Invent Him," in *The Don Juan Papers: Further Castaneda Controversies*, ed. Richard de Mille (Belmont, Calif.: Wadsworth Publishing, 1990), 254.

24. Reno, "If Don Juan Did Not Exist," 258.

25. Marton, "Castaneda's Legacy," 275.

26. Marton, "Castaneda's Legacy," 285.

27. Marton, "Castaneda's Legacy," 286.

28. Runyan Castaneda, *Magical Journey*, 25.

29. Runyan Castaneda, *Magical Journey*, 81.

30. Runyan Castaneda, *Magical Journey*, 92–93.

31. Runyan Castaneda, *Magical Journey*, 99.

32. Carlos Castaneda, *The Eagle's Gift* (New York: Simon and Schuster, 1981), 175.

33. Runyan Castaneda, *Magical Journey*, 100–101.

34. Runyan Castaneda, *Magical Journey*, 92–93.

35. Runyan Castaneda, *Magical Journey*, 111.

36. C. Roderick Wilson, "Seeing They See Not," in *Being Changed: The Anthropology of Extraordinary Experience*, ed. David. E. Young and Jean-Guy Goulet (Ontario, Canada: Broadview Press, 1994), 201.

37. Harner, *Shaman*, xx.

38. De Mille, "Shaman," 19.

39. Quoted in Runyan Castaneda, *Magical Journey*, 88–90.

40. Runyan Castaneda, *Magical Journey*, 103.

41. Runyan Castaneda, *Magical Journey*, 122.

42. Quoted in Runyan Castaneda, *Magical Journey*, 122.

43. Runyan Castaneda, *Magical Journey*, 171–172.

44. Runyan Castaneda, *Magical Journey*, 171.

45. Runyan Castaneda, *Magical Journey*, 128–129.

46. Marton, "Castaneda's Legacy," 281.

47. Jean-Guy Goulet, "Dreams and Visions in Other Lifeworlds," in *Being Changed: The Anthropology of Extraordinary Experience*, ed. David. E. Young and Jean-Guy Goulet (Ontario, Canada: Broadview Press, 1994) 16–17.

48. Runyan Castaneda, *Magical Journey*, 166–167.

49. Castaneda, *Eagle's Gift*, 7–8.

50. Carlos Castaneda, *Journey to Ixtlan: The Lessons of Don Juan* (New York: Pocket Books, 1974), 191.

51. Reno, "If Don Juan Did Not Exist," 255.

52. Claude Lévi-Strauss, *Structural Anthropology* (New York: Basic Books, 1963), 175.

53. Castaneda, *Ixtlan*, viii.

54. Carlos Castaneda, *The Power of Silence: Further Lessons of Don Juan* (New York: Simon and Schuster, 1987), 9.

55. Carlos Castaneda, *Active Side of Infinity* (New York: Harper Perennial, 2000), 69.

56. Carlos Castaneda, *The Art of Dreaming* (New York: Harper Perennial, 1994), vii.

57. Harner, *Shaman*, xxiii.

58. Mircea Eliade, *Rites and Symbols of Initiation: The Mysteries of Birth and Rebirth* (1958; reprint, New York: Harper & Row, 1975), 95.

59. Castaneda, *Silence*, 10.

60. Castaneda, *Ixtlan*, 194.

61. Carlos Castaneda, *The Second Ring of Power* (New York: Simon and Schuster, 1977), 271.

62. Carlos Castaneda, *Tales of Power* (New York: Pocket Books), 109.

63. Carlos Castaneda, *The Fire from Within* (New York: Pocket Books, 1984), 37.

64. Harner, *Shaman*, 46.

65. Eliade, *Rites*, 38.

66. Castaneda, *Fire Within*, 41–42.

67. Carlos Castaneda, *The Teachings of Don Juan: A Yaqui Way of Knowledge* (New York: Ballantine Books, 1968), 77.

68. Harner, *Shaman*, xxiv.

69. Harner, *Shaman*, 44.

70. Eliade, *Rites*, 87.

71. Castaneda, *Silence*, 12.

72. Castaneda, *Teachings*, thirtieth anniversary ed. (1968; reprint, New York: Washington Square Press, 1998), xiii–xiv.

73. Castaneda, *Silence*, 10.

74. Castaneda, *Silence*, 11.

75. Castaneda, *Silence*, 13.

76. Marie Francoise Guédon, "Dene Ways and the Ethnographer's Culture," in *Being Changed: The Anthropology of Extraordinary Experience*, ed. David. E. Young and Jean-Guy Goulet (Ontario, Canada: Broadview Press, 1994), 50.

77. Guédon, "Dene Ways," 51.

78. Castaneda, *Tales*, 236.

79. Castaneda, *Ixtlan*, ix.

80. Holger Kalweit, *Dreamtime and Inner Space: The World of the Shaman* (Boston: Shambala, 1998), 226.

81. Kalweit, *Dreamtime*, 119.

82. Castaneda, *Tales*, 107.

83. Castaneda, *Tales*, 154.

84. Castaneda, *Infinity*, 1.

85. Castaneda, *Tales*, 238.

86. Castaneda, *Tales*, 239.

87. Randall Collins, *Three Sociological Traditions* (New York: Oxford University Press, 1985), 157.

88. Castaneda, *Ixtlan*, 194.

89. Bruce Lincoln, *Discourse and the Construction of Society: Comparative Studies of Myth, Ritual, and Classification* (New York: Oxford University Press, 1989), 53.

90. Holger Kalweit, *Shamans, Healers, and Medicine Men* (Boston: Shambala, 1992), 162.

91. Kalweit, *Dreamtime*, 95.

92. Kalweit, *Dreamtime*, 163.

93. Guédon, "Dene Ways," 39.

94. Peter McLaren, *Schooling as a Ritual Performance: Toward a Political Economy of Educational Symbols and Gestures* (New York: Routledge, 1993), 37.

95. Castaneda, *Ixtlan*, 168.

96. Castaneda, *Tales*, 178.

97. Emile Durkheim, *The Elementary Forms of the Religious Life* (1915; reprint, New York: Free Press, 1965), 417–418.

98. Eliade, *Rites*, x–xi.

99. Roger C. Schank, *Tell Me a Story* (Evanston, Ill.: Northwestern University Press, 1990), 219.

100. Kalweit, *Dreamtime*, 94.

101. Kalweit, *Shaman*, 4.

102. Castaneda, *Ixtlan*, 267.

103. Castaneda, *Tales*, 247.

104. Castaneda, *Gift*, 9.

105. Castaneda, *Tales*, 249.

106. Kalweit, *Shaman*, 103.

107. Kalweit, *Dreamtime*, 145.

108. Castaneda, *Ixtlan*, xiii.

109. Castaneda, *Silence*, 11.

## Chapter Five

# The Silent Curriculum: A Case Study

The only reason (the Soto [Zen] priests say) that the Rinzai [Zen] training uses koans [spiritual riddles] almost continuously is because Rinzai attracts intellectual, or merely restless, minds. To force a restless mind to sit and concentrate on the great "Nothing" that causes and explains all phenomena is impossible. So the Rinzai disciple has to be tricked, and he is tricked by giving him koans to solve. With a koan he is under the impression that he has "something to do."

Janwillem van de Wetering, *A Glimpse of Nothingness: Experiences in an American Zen Community* (New York: Washington Square Press, 1975), 99.

This case study research was undertaken to investigate the practical application of the ideas presented in the preceding chapters of this book. Although the study was undertaken according to formal academic protocols, I will present it in this chapter without the procedural detail that would be required in a strictly academic presentation. In this chapter, we will examine how a *silent curriculum* that teaches the all-important *silent knowledge* discussed by don Juan plays out in the education of contemporary computer professionals.

The study attempts to investigate the construction of professional meaning for computer students in this program. Schön demonstrates that student success demands mastery of elements that cannot be directly taught or learned. He indicates that the difficulty in transmitting this indirect knowledge is the fault of neither the instructor nor the student. Teachers cannot directly communicate their knowledge to students because it is impossible to simplify the essential complexity of that knowledge to a student's level.

101

Students find it impossible to immediately understand teachers because language is inadequate to directly convey the underlying framework suggested by that knowledge. This study explores alternative ways to describe and discuss this teaching/learning process.

This ethnographic case study involved a Computer Information Systems (CIS) department at a small, midwestern liberal arts college with a Catholic heritage. The study included the gathering of documentation (including the college catalog, department admissions brochures, course syllabi, and assignments), in-depth interviews with all CIS faculty and a range of CIS students including freshmen through program graduates, and field observations in settings frequented by CIS faculty and students (including the computer lab and CIS classes). Only a subset of the supporting evidence of the full academic study will be presented in this chapter. Actual names of individuals participating in the study have been omitted or altered, and personally identifying information has been omitted to protect privacy.

## THE OFFICIAL CURRICULUM

A Computer Information Systems program is different than a Computer Science program. Computer Science (CS) graduates normally work for computer hardware and software manufacturers, concentrating on the machine and its electronic components. Computer Information Systems graduates normally work for a business that uses the hardware and software produced by CS graduates. CIS graduates typically enter business organizations as programmers or programmer/analysts and tend to move quickly into systems analysts positions. Systems analysts examine business information problems and set up both computer and procedural solutions to those problems. The following CIS professor helps to clarify the nature of the professional work a Computer Information Systems graduate does.

Instead of studying about the computer itself, you're going to study about how computers are used to help somebody else get information. . . . I think that Computer Science traditionally has been building better cars and Computer Information Systems has been saying we're going to buy a better a car and teach somebody how to make good use of it. . . . If you think about the army, the army has lots of ways they use computers. [One] need would be to use computers to figure out how to get a Patriot missile close to an incoming missile. That's more computer science and computer engineering. But figuring out the logistics of how many people, how many K-rations you need a week, and if you need 50,000 K-rations a week, how many ships do you need—that's the information needs. (Dr. A)

Freshman CIS students initially focus on application software, such as word processors, spreadsheets, databases, and graphics and communication programs. Most traditional students entering the major from high schools have had some experience with such software. Nontraditional students transferring into the major from other programs typically have exposure to this type of software through introductory computer courses required by their original majors.

> The very first thing is they start getting used to what computers can do; it starts when they are a freshman before they learn to program. (Dr. A)

Sophomore students move from the application software environment to actually writing simple application programs in programming classes. Though the department places less emphasis on programming than it did just a few years ago, graduates still often enter an organization through a position that requires them to program, first as a "maintenance" programmer, rewriting portions of existing programs, and later as a programmer/analyst, writing larger modules of original programs. Even as they advance into systems analyst roles, understanding programming provides them with an essential knowledge base.

> I think [students] have to know how to write a program. They absolutely have to know that . . . they're going to be trying to help people use computers to improve their organization, and, fundamentally, it comes down to what can be programmed into a computer. . . . You need a feel for how hard the job is that you're talking about; how hard is it going to be to get the computer to do what it is that you want it do. . . . Typically what a Computer Information Systems person does is to go into an office where a person wants to do something new to get more information. At the end of that interview, you have to know whether it's feasible to do it. (Dr. A)

In the junior year, students begin their study of systems analysis and design. The sequence of courses teaches students how to analyze an existing management system, to improve existing systems, and to design new ones. The senior year continues this process by introducing appropriate new technologies and by placing students in an internship to gain practical experience. The junior and senior courses, the ones that emphasize analysis and design over programming, are the real professional emphasis of departmental curriculum.

## THE SILENT CURRICULUM

An implicit, *silent* curriculum quietly coexists within the official curriculum. The official curriculum focuses on the importance of programming languages and systems design work, but the principal elements of an implicit world view curriculum are identified as: 1) an ability to adapt and deal with the incredible pace of change in the industry, 2) an ability to construct a model or frame with which to visualize computer concepts, and 3) an ability to solve technical and human problems of an organization that revolve around the use of a computer.

### Change and Adaptability

A computer professional cannot merely prepare for that which currently exists. The rate of change is too swift and too certain. Application software and programming languages learned as a student are commonly obsolete upon graduation. Capitalism fuels the relentless (and profitable) march of technological change that in turn fuels a need for computer professionals to constantly adjust to that change.

Computer hardware itself develops at a phenomenal rate. New microchip designs and manufacturing processes continue to make everything smaller, cheaper, and more reliable. The microcomputer on the typical desk is much more powerful than the original mainframes that required space the size of a house. Computers themselves are now used to design the newer chips. Computer software change builds on the increased speed and capacity of hardware change and in turn creates a demand for yet more speed and capacity. Computer hardware and software sales revolve around profitable cycles of planned obsolescence. Each stage in the evolution of the technology involves more speed, more power, more features, and more ease. The hardware and software dance a dizzying dervish around each other.

Much of what is taught about hardware and software changes quickly. Programming languages come into and fall out of favor. I complained one day to a friend who taught in a religious studies department about the difficulty of staying abreast of all this change. "I knew there were advantages to teaching Old Testament," he quipped.

I think that in the computer field there's just so much change that's required, and change requires that you be able to quickly learn something new. That requires a certain level of ability. (Dr. A)

You need to be very adaptable in this profession. Slick on your feet. Be able to take on a new challenge without fear. (Dr. B)

Change is entirely important. The computers we're using, that we will use in the [future], are just not being made right now. The programs that we will have our freshman using in the [future], have not been announced off the drawing board yet. (Dr. C)

A lot of the stuff that you learn at school doesn't apply to the job directly. The computer language C, that I used on the job . . . I never had a course in it. I was never taught that language. All the hardware we worked with . . . I had never been taught. A lot of the structures . . . I'd never seen before. But I was taught concepts that I could apply so well to that. I was taught structured programming and Pascal structured programming. It's amazing. (Dr. D)

## FRAMES AND VISUALIZATION

As the specifics of computer professional education are destined for quick obsolescence, the emphasis of the major would seem to rely on the underlying principles of computing. However, as if in some sort of postmodern nightmare, even fundamental principles change routinely in computer design and practice. What is left is the need to develop frames capable of visualizing and engaging temporal technological truths. Equally important, practitioners need to develop ways of checking their existing frames for inadequacy and modifying them as needed.

> I think that good programmers have mental pictures; they have a model. I think that bad programmers don't get this model, and so when they try to write a program, they don't picture what's happening physically. They don't see it in the back of their mind as something that every one of these statements is doing. (Dr. A)

> Visualization can be a very significant part of it. How to visualize and how to make that work for them from where they're coming from . . . connecting things and then building upon that and connecting new things. (Dr. B)

> you learn all these individual things, and it creates some sort of framework in your mind. You're really not going to rely on those individual components; you're going to rely on this framework of thinking in your mind when you're handling a problem or doing something. . . . Anything our students learn now is going to be obsolete by the time they leave here. (Dr. D)

## PROBLEM SOLVING

By the time CIS students graduate, they need to understand that the essential task of the curriculum is to think and to deal with the human and technical problems that abound in contemporary institutions. This ability becomes embodied in the term *problem solving*.

> you could put a chunk in here, you can put a chunk in there . . . but my feeling is that in virtually any curriculum that has something to do with computers, it's going to be unavoidable that the students are going to run into problems. . . . The people that survive or thrive on that are the people that can see their way through a problem and find a solution. . . . People who survive the CIS courses, no matter how you lay them out, how you divide them up, what you put in here, what you put in there . . . if they're going to survive what-

ever the requirements are in the curriculum, they're going to end up with the ability to analyze or think their way out of a problem. (Dr. C)

This facet of the silent curriculum explicitly demonstrates what Schön continually points out. The very thing the curriculum identifies as essential to student success is itself frustratingly elusive and indirect for both students and their teachers.

I see some bright students who are able to answer all the questions, but again, they've just taken what you've given them, and they're studying that really hard, and they are able to answer the questions. I don't think that that's enough. . . . I really think that good, bright active students get it and dull, less active students don't ever get it. I think, in general, it just really depends on how mentally active a person is, and I don't know that it's teachable. . . . I don't know how we would teach it, or enforce it, or measure whether they've learned it. (Dr. A)

we don't tackle it [problem solving] specifically. We talk about it a lot, but one good example of problem solving is to say, let's go through the systems analysis, design, and implementation sequence of three courses. (Dr. B)

[It is vitally important] to go through a methodology that assures you that you know what the problem is. To be able to translate that, you don't get all that out of a curriculum. (Dr. B)

CIS professors candidly view student mastery of problem solving as something students simply are or are not able to master. After reviewing research on problem solving, and after experimenting with untold approaches and techniques, faculty have concluded that nothing they do seems to make any difference in whether a student becomes an effective problem solver. They see problem solving as something that cannot be taught. Successful upperclassmen adopt their professors' views and join them in communicating it downward to aspiring freshmen and sophomores. These beliefs form a framework that revolves around the key elements of *time* and *work*.

Time and work. That's how it was when I was in school. To understand a lot of things, you actually have to do them, or at least use the approach in a lot of computers. . . . You can have that theory explained to you, but it doesn't make sense until you make it your own and create with it. You can't have a programming language explained. It's like any language. (Dr. D)

## THE SHAMAN CURRICULUM

A gap exists between the explicit, official curriculum and the implicit, silent curriculum. The official curriculum is the one that conscientious departments continually examine and revise and that university curriculum committees study under magnifying lenses in turf-conscious detail. Yet the silent curriculum contains the more important concepts, behaviors, and skills that a department expects graduates to understand and exhibit. Ironically, the all-important silent curriculum is not explicitly addressed by departments, and it is not presented to or approved by any curriculum committee because it is essentially invisible to faculty for whom it is such an internalized part of themselves. Faculty basically do not recognize it as a curriculum and are unaware that they are teaching it between the lines of the curriculum they view as important. The remainder of this chapter is an attempt to make explicit the teaching of the silent curriculum. The Shaman's Strategy (see figure 4.1) presented in the previous chapter is used as a frame in which to develop the Shaman's Curriculum (see figure 5.1) of this CIS program.

### Hooking and Misdirection

Students seldom enter the CIS program with a realistic awareness of the nature of the work they can expect to do upon graduation. Students enter the program with endless preconceptions based on what they already like to do with computers and on what other uninitiated individuals have told them about computer work. This lack of realism is evident even when students have been explicitly informed about such work. The words simply do not mean much to the uninitiated. Moreover, it is doubtful that an accurate understanding of professional work would be a significant enticement to students at the early stages of their programs. Students in contemporary professional programs are characteristically looking at education as a means to "get their ticket punched"; virtually no one seems eager to significantly change the way they view reality. As a result, it is easy to demon-

1. **Hooking and Misdirection:** Students are lured into the program by their own preconceptions, and the explicit curricular activities misdirect attention from the implicit curriculum.
   a) Students are "hooked" by their "ordinary world" preconceptions (and misconceptions) of professional computer work.
   b) Student attention is misdirected with pseudotasks from world view construction to the explicit activities of the formal curriculum, as if those activities were the main goal of their education.
2. **Ritual and Myth:** Students are "tricked" into constructing a professional identity framed around a technological, problem-solving world view; preconceptions are subtly dismantled and replaced by a broader "professional" world view.
   a) Through ritual activity, students are tricked into adopting a new world view, learning to act "as if" they are already professionals, and they bind themselves to the group and separate themselves from "ordinary" people.
   b) Through the transmission of stories, especially through informal conversation with "initiated" members, students learn to focus and frame their cognitive attention.
3. **World View Reconstruction:** Many students go through a process of loss and renewal; they are intuitively aware that their world view reconstruction may incur certain loss. Some students have more to lose than others.

**Figure 5.1   The Shaman's Curriculum (The Shaman's Strategy Applied to CIS Apprentices)**

strate that students are "hooked" into the program by a combination of their own preconceptions and of the courses featured early in the program that encourage those preconceptions.

Freshmen and sophomores seem blissfully unaware of the stated intent of the program despite an abundance of both oral and written descriptions. Instead, their constructions appear to be influenced almost exclusively by the type of activity toward which the explicit curriculum moves them. Freshmen and sophomores, who primarily work with application software (e.g., word processing, spreadsheets, databases, graphics, network e-mail, and programming languages), universally view the computer profession from a standpoint of such software; this is especially true for students who work as computer lab assistants.

Besides application programs, freshmen and sophomores are also introduced to basic hardware and software concepts and quickly develop a basic computer vocabulary. The speech of the first- and second-year students is strewn with application software references. This enhances their working vocabulary and begins the process of separating them from nonmajors. Many of them value the hands-on time in the lab and barely acknowledge the classroom portion of their education.

we went over Norton Utilities and that's really useful, I think, and then some
of the information on videos, the graphics, and capabilities of certain graphics, I felt that was pretty interesting. I really haven't taken too many classes
that taught anything really specific other than how to use DOS and Windows and things like that. I'd say the biggest thing I've learned this year was
from working around computers. (freshman)

Mirroring the "hooking" of apprentices by shamans, freshmen are
"hooked" into the major. For some, the hook was set in high school
classes, when they decided to pursue a computer career, but in this particular program, most students are hooked from the ranks of other majors
while taking required computer classes and from the ranks of students exploring various career possibilities. Much of this learning is foundational
and becomes background to CIS majors' future work.

[CorelDraw] can make really neat graphics and things. . . It's pretty exhila-
rating to make something neat with that, design some pictures or what have
you. Another thing is using Unix to do file transfers to bring both programs
up on your computer from Washington or Oregon or something like that. It's
really great. (freshman)

Beginning students' career expectations reflect a software-use bias and,
if they work in the lab, they closely align their expectations to their lab assistant work.

I train students and faculty on how to use software applications like Quattro Pro, WordPerfect or Windows . . . that kind of stuff. (sophomore)

Most of the jobs around here would be to work for a business, working with
the people maintaining a network for them or maybe maintaining all their
computers to keep them working. (freshman)

In actuality, neither of these quotes accurately reflects the work of a
systems analyst. The former role would be the job of a software trainer;
the latter would be the job of a computer operator or technician, either of
whom would be vocational school graduates.

I would like something that I do now in the lab and that would be something
like consulting. I've also thought about programming. . . . If I could be a pro-

grammer or a system analyst that is kind of the title to go for I think . . . from what I've read, what they do is they program and they watch the mainframe. Kind of like keeping up to date and things like that. (sophomore)

This sophomore construction expands the freshman view to include programming. It is different in that he is interested in the "kind of title to go for"; however, he, too has an inaccurate understanding of what someone with that title actually does. Systems analysts do not "watch the mainframe"; such a task is another that would be assigned to a computer operator, a two-year vocational graduate.

Sophomores, who face the "weed-out" courses, C Programming and Advanced C Programming, begin to view mastery of programming languages rather than application software as a major goal of the curriculum. These two courses get their attention, as the courses are regarded as "weed-out" courses by faculty and students alike.

My big kick . . . is helping write software, working with computer products that really help people . . . that excites me. (sophomore)

Students who successfully complete the programming sequence have been successfully "hooked" and quickly find that their education to this point fades into the background and is taken for granted. This is not the only strategy being carried out at this time. From the very onset of the hooking process, the program also begins to instill in the unsuspecting apprentice the basic elements of the silent curriculum. The "hook" is used to move students from the frame provided by their preconceptions toward something that is beyond their ability to frame realistically. Students are aware that they are being trained to be systems analysts; they simply do not have a realistic notion of what systems analysts actually do.

It is important to note that hooking is not a devious Machiavellian process. Students are simply pursuing a career path that they believe they understand. Faculty are simply providing a gentle introduction to the profession. On a conscious level, it allows students to explore whether this is a path they wish to take; it allows faculty to judge whether this is a path on which the student has a chance of being successful. Beyond this, it is a fundamentally unconscious process that gently leads students down a path with heart. It is a process that draws students into the deeper, secret world view of this profession.

## Misdirection

The essential indirect learning of the silent curriculum becomes a by-product of the less essential learning of the explicit curriculum. It is not that the explicit curriculum is unimportant; it is simply incomplete. The formal curriculum beguiles students into believing that mastery of the formal curriculum is the goal of their education. While a given programming course gives the impression that learning that particular language is inherently important, the silent curriculum beneath teaches a type of problem solving that can be accessed in various facets of a computer professional's life. Even as computer assignments, tests, and grades focus student attention on the activities of the formal curriculum, students are weaving themselves into the fabric of a professional world view.

This misdirection begins in teaching students to use commercial software, such as the Norton Utilities. In a Hardware/Software Concepts class assignment designed to teach students to use the Norton Utilities software (see figure 5.2), students are indeed prepared to make sophisticated use of a sophisticated application program. But the assignment also helps students to develop a professional vocabulary and world view. Besides learning to successfully use this program, a student who completes this assignment will have been introduced to essential disk storage vocabulary and concepts and to the ideas that professional mastery requires *play* and more than a perfunctory completion of an assignment. A side benefit is that students who recover lost disk files for someone who is uninitiated into the mysteries of this software may experience additional benefits by being accorded deferential (even reverential) status.

The programming assignment (see figure 5.3) illustrates a similar principle, as it is applied to the writing of programs. This assignment offers problems in the use of single and double dimensional arrays (also called *tables*). From a formal curriculum perspective, the important thing a student is learning here is how to use sets of the correct problem-solving steps (called *algorithms*) to create solutions for the problems presented. From a silent curriculum perspective, it is more helpful to view these problems as repetitions of basic concepts that require increasingly sophisticated visualization and the building of a world view toolbox of potential solutions to use for larger, more sophisticated problems.

Use the <u>Norton Utilities Lost Files Disk</u> you received in class to do this assignment. You will be recovering several erased/lost disk files. Do yourself a favor and do more than merely try to finish this assignment. PLAY! This is one program that you can't know too much about. PLAY! It's really okay to do that.

1. Access the Novell network in the lab. Type "CIS" to access the CIS department file server. Choose drive A.
2. Type "NORTON" to access the Norton Integrator program.
3. Select the Norton Utilities option using drive A.
4. Use the Norton Explore Disk options to answer the following:
   A. What files appear in the file listing?
   B. What are the starting clusters of the following files? Which are hidden files?
      ibmdos.com →
      ibmbio.com →
      command.com →
   C. What sectors do the following occupy?
      boot      →
      FAT       →
      Root Dir  →
   D. What is the disk label (name) and where is it stored?
   E. What are directory entries 5–8 and their starting cluster #s?
5. Unerase the two deleted files (named lonshark.com and hogs.txt).
6. Search and recover a file that has been lost rather than erased. Search data portion for the word "INSURANCE" (in UPPERCASE). Find which clusters are involved and write those clusters into a file.
7. Search the data portion of the disk for another lost file. This file contains a questionnaire for you to find and write into a file.
8. Exit the NU program and use the Speed Disk program (available through the Norton Integrator or by typing SD) to organize all of the files on your diskette into contiguous files.
9. Exit the Norton Utilities and print the four ASCII files that you unerased/recovered to the printer (COPY filename.ext LPT1).
10. Turn in your printouts *and* your disk.

**Figure 5.2   Norton Utilities Assignment**

The ability to solve large problems results from developing solutions for a variety of small problems. The problems presented for solution in this assignment have no practical application; they are analogous to finger exercises for someone learning to play a piano. Their intent is to develop explicit programming skill, but they develop as well the conceptual requirements to deal with programming tables of any kind. The curricular trick used is to assign enough problems so that connections are made between them. Again, the implicit message is that even with the multitude of different kinds of problems, unless students do more than the assigned work, the connections made may not be adequate to ensure that the goals of the silent curriculum are being met.

1. Write a program to read a fifty-character record from a file into an array and search the array to count the number of times the letter E occurs in it. Print the number of E occurrences for each record until you reach the end of the file.
2. Write a program that reads an eighty-character record from a file and counts the number of times each letter of the alphabet occurs in the text, storing the counts in an array. Print the count for each letter with an identifying label.
3. **Hint:** Use a second array containing letters of the alphabet to do the comparisons. Suppose the first letter of the alphabet is C. This letter is found in the third position of the alphabet array; one should then be added to the third position of the count array.
4. You are given a text of fifteen characters. Place these characters in an array and print them. Rotate the characters one position to the left and print them again; repeat this process twenty times.
   GODFATHER LIVES
   ODFATHER LIVESG
   DFATHER LIVESGO
   FATHER LIVESGOD
   etc.
5. Repeat problem #3, but rotate characters to the right.
6. Two arrays of twenty elements each contain numbers in the range from −99 to +99. Write a program that determines which pairs (if any) add up to 50. A pair consists of one element from each array. For example, the following might be true:
   array1(3) = 25      array2(18) = 25      (total = 50)
   array1(5) = 99      array2(14) = −49      (total = 50)
   **Hint:** Start with the first element of the first array and pair it with each element of the second array. Then pair the second element of the first array with each element of the second array, etc.

**Figure 5.3    Array/Table Assignment**

This implicit reality of the silent curriculum routinely surfaces in assignments. Professors often develop an implicit assignment within an explicit one. Such an assignment typically "tricks" students into thinking the prescribed activity is the important part of the assignment even though the professor views it merely a means to an end. Students may even think the assignment is idiotic, as they aren't told and don't understand its intended purpose.

For example, one freshman assignment (see figure 5.4) was intended to acquaint students with the wide range of information available to Internet users and to provide practice in utilizing many different approaches to locating that Internet information. Although students might surmise that the professor really is interested in stock prices or Congressional bills, any computer teacher looking at the list is likely to immediately recognize its real purpose. Interestingly, the professor designated the last item as extra credit when he himself was unable to find the requested information. He said, "I assume if I

Give the URL (Uniform Resource Locator) of the following resources. Give any other information requested.

1. Find an audio clip of a greeting from President Clinton.
2. Find a current weather map.
3. Give the current stock market prices for the following stocks: IBM, Apple, and AT&T.
4. Give two articles from a daily newspaper. Give the title of each article and its URL.
5. Find the map of the Emory University Law Library. Tell what is located in the room to the right of the first floor main entrance.
6. Find the infant mortality rate of a country whose name begins with the first letter of your last name. (**Hint:** try the files of a U.S. spy agency.)
7. Find the population of a state. Also give the populations of the three largest racial groups in that state.
8. Find a music file. (**Hint:** There is a Captain Kirk Singalong home page.)
9. Get a preview movie clip for the movie *Junior*.
10. List three bills that have been submitted to the 103rd U.S. Congress dealing with the Internet.
11. Get a picture of the Shoemaker–Levy comet hitting Jupiter.
12. Find a listing for a computer job in Asia.
Extra Credit:
Find the name of a wheelchair accessible bookstore in Berkeley, California.

**Figure 5.4    Internet Assignment**

couldn't find it, students wouldn't be able to find it either. What I really wanted was just to have them try. They will learn a lot in just trying." Despite the obviousness of the silent assignment, few professors would consciously frame the assignment within a larger silent curriculum. To reframe it as such would move the focus beyond the purpose of a particular assignment within a course to the purpose of a particular course within a curriculum.

The case study assignment (see figure 5.5) reflects how junior-level assignments differ from freshman-level assignments and how the silent curriculum is intensified. This case requires students to play the role of hospital information systems managers facing an important decision. Should the hospital reconfigure the current information system's treatment of requisitions in line with Internet protocols, or wait to see what the next "wrinkle" in relevant technology offers? The instructor's caveat that "there are no 'right' answers" underscores the brave new world into which the upper-division student is being thrust. Not only are there multiple "right" answers, but the criteria for correctness is being altered subtly, as the analyst must also expect rapid obsolescence. To a large extent, this obsolescence stems from technical innovation, but it also results from the mysterious realm of business mergers, acquisitions, and product strategies. The combination of these factors means that a "solution" that is no longer on the technological cutting edge may remain "right" for strategic reasons.

Also, although not directly mentioned in this assignment, a particular organization's internal structures may alter the suitability of a particular "solution." Thus, assignments like those exhibited in figure 5.5 teach students to understand technology as time- and context-specific. Today's acceptable solution might become a "problem" when new technologies make it anachronistic, or when the technical or organizational assumptions on which it relies are superseded.

This assignment reinforces several areas of the silent curriculum. It emphasizes the fast pace of technological change and the need to adapt. It requires the ability to frame and visualize the complexity of temporal technological truth. And it requires complex, real-life problem solving. It does all this while leaving students with the impression that this particular assignment and their particular solutions are of importance.

---

Read through the "Baxter International: OnCall as Soon as Possible?" case study. Unlike the previous case study, this one does not present a clear question to the reader. I would like you to take the role of an MIS manager at a hospital who has recently learned about the OnCall system. Assume your hospital currently does not use any EDI* methods for purchasing. Do you think your hospital should move to the new system now? Should the hospital wait a while and see if the Internet changes how EDI is conducted? What are the main advantages/disadvantages of the new system?

Be aware that this case study is a couple of years old. In that time, control of OnCall has been passed from Baxter to a company called TSI (I think Baxter may also have spun off TSI). You should look at some current information about OnCall at the TSI web page:

- Overview of TSI's OnCall
- Frequently Asked Questions (FAQs) Regarding OnCall*EDI

Remember that we already read one article about EDI over the Internet that mentioned OnCall:

- "New Life for EDI? The Internet May Help Electronic Data Interchange Finally Meet Expectations," *Information Week*, 17 March 1997.

Read at least two of the position papers from other students and post at least one response to the discussion board.

Remember, as you discuss others' work, that we are not dealing with simple black and white issues here and that there is no "right" answer—though each of us is entitled to his or her opinion as to which answers are better than others.

---
* Electronic Data Interchange. EDI is the transmission, in a standardized syntax, of business information between computers of independent companies or organizations.

**Figure 5.5   Systems Analysis and Design Case Study**

## Ritual and Myth

From a Durkheimian perspective, the inherent pedagogic rituals of education are specific ways of focusing a student's attention and emotions. Ritual focuses the body's attention toward an explicit curriculum while subtly encoding messages from the silent curriculum. Such a perspective can be viewed in this program. Through the secular rituals of class attendance, assignments, tests, and lab interaction, attention is focused on the external manifestations of what it means to be a computer professional while quietly constructing a foundation to support a professional world view. The student who fully participates in these rituals generally becomes thoroughly immersed in the world view of the silent curriculum.

As students in this computer department progress through the four-year program, they construct and reconstruct a series of world view frames that give meaning to their experiences and define their future professional goals. When asked what they expect to do after completing their majors, students tend to answer in terms of what they have already done or are presently doing. Although they often use the correct terms to discuss what they expect to do upon graduation, their comments disclose that they do not understand what those terms mean in actual practice. This is particularly true in the early stages of learning. Those apprentices who master the silent curriculum seem to do so by absorbing the ritual and myth of the program.

### Ritual Activity

I realized that almost imperceptibly the lab sites elicited certain forms of action and discouraged others.

Sharon Traweek, *Beamtimes and Lifetimes: The World of High Energy Physicists* (Cambridge: Harvard University Press, 1988), x.

For Goffman, ritual is essential because it maintains our confidence in basic social relationships. It provides others with opportunities to affirm the legitimacy of our position in the social structure while obliging us to do the same. Ritual is a placement mechanism in which, for the most part, social inferiors affirm the higher positions of their superiors.[1]

Although several key outcomes occur as a result of participation in ritual activity, we will be primarily concerned with only two of them. One outcome is that certain types of language and action embodied by professionals have been promoted while others not embodied by professionals have been discouraged. A second outcome is that group members have been bound together while simultaneously being separated from nonmembers. We could also use Durkheim's concepts and say that the purpose is to bind together the sacred and distinguish it from the profane, or we could use Castaneda's concepts and say that the purpose is to bind together the warriors and to distinguish them from ordinary people. The previously described hooking/misdirection strategy is tightly woven into ritual activity. Both of these ritual outcomes are fundamentally invisible to students who continue to focus their attention on the explicit lab tasks. Ritual is, in essence, a reality-changing trick to induce students to act as if they were already the professionals they seek to become.

Although ritual activity is evident throughout the program in classes and virtually all student–faculty and student–student interactions, the naked power of ritual is most observable in the computer labs. The structure of the computer labs themselves and the lab interactions of computer majors with each other and with nonmajors contribute to the ritual outcomes. The lab layout clearly transmits to computer majors that they have certain prerogatives not afforded nonmajors. The lab interaction of nonmajors with the majors also affords them a special status unique to this setting. In the labs, CIS majors are afforded clear views of the professional world, are bound together with other majors and separated from ordinary students, and are afforded a look at the social professional milieu in which they will shortly operate.

The computer lab is actually a whole floor in a wing of the main building on the campus. It contains four separate lab areas designed for general and classroom use and for specific CIS projects. Lab assistants, most of whom are CIS majors, are employed in the lab area. It is their job to assign computers to students and faculty who wish to use the lab, to answer general questions, and to help solve student hardware and software problems. Lab assistants guide most students into the general-use "Micro" lab, thereby keeping unsophisticated users out of the "Systems" lab used for CIS classes. The hardware and some of the software in the Systems lab are more sophisticated than those in the general lab. The full-time staff lab supervisor told me that the typical student "would be intimidated" by the Systems lab.

The general Micro lab is usually very busy. At one end of the lab, tables contain eight specialty computers. This is essentially an area set up for CIS majors. One side of the table contains multimedia computers that use special graphic software and CD technology; they are seldom used by anyone except CIS majors. The other side of this table contains computers that are effectively the personal computers of individual CIS majors; each is a testament to the individual's standing within the department. Each of these computers has a sign on it. During one of my observations, two said, "Please Do Not Disturb." One said, "Bryan's Gopher Server"; another had a sign that said, "Scott's Workstation." None of these computers was turned on. The signs resembled a canine-style marking of territory.

Another whole table next to these computers is used as a repair area. Computers on this table sit open in various states of disrepair. The act of sitting near piles of computer interface cards and wires is apparently a part of the professional process. CIS student prerogative in this specialty computer area and in the Systems lab is obvious. They seem to exist as areas that fit the Durkheimian notion of the "sacred." Reserved for the priests and the priest-apprentices, these form sacred areas in the computer temple, accessible and comfortable only to the initiated, inspiring awe and discomfort in the uninitiated.

Majors who help others utilize terminology cues to assess another student's membership in the group and to gauge how much work will be required to assist a person. These terminology cues work to establish a personal professional identity as well as to bind an individual to the CIS group while simultaneously reducing the person being helped to the status of an ordinary person.

One of the biggest [keys to determining whether another person knows anything about computers] is terminology. . . . For instance, if somebody says my monitor's not working or the local network is not working right, now then it sounds like they know something about it, and you can work with them in solving the problem. If they say my computer doesn't work, then that's a bad sign. (freshman)

Freshmen and sophomores use terminology cues almost exclusively to judge the interest and skill levels of those with whom they interact.

Calling hardware components by their assigned ("correct") names is essential. It helps lab assistants and majors to gauge the extent of a problem. If someone erroneously calls a 3½" disk a hard disk (because its case is plastic), a helper is alerted to be very specific in explanations because that student doesn't know what a hard disk really is and will get easily confused.

> [I can tell how much someone knows by] they way they ask. The terms they use . . . A lot of times people will call the hard drive, hard disk. The major one is not understanding that the 3½" disk is a floppy disk . . . certain people you explain what it is and certain people you just tell them, this is how you fix it. Because some people you can just tell they ask me what it is and you can just see the difference in whether they really want to know or they just want to get rid of it. . . . Just the way they ask a question. It clues you in. (junior)

The "floppy disk" reference of this student indicates the power of terminology in an apprenticeship as well as the subtle manner in which professional myths tie into ritual. To the uninitiated, it is confusing to call a 3½" disk "floppy" because, having a hard plastic shell, it doesn't flop. To the initiated, the term has a historical and denotative significance that transcends its physical characteristics. Antecedents to the 3½" disk were literally floppy, and the term was chosen to distinguish such a disk from the nonremovable "hard" or "fixed" disk installed inside the computer. Although *removable disk* may have been a preferable term to *floppy*, that distinction would still be problematic today because some current hard/fixed disks are also removable. The historical context of terminology thus forms an important aspect of the computer professional mythology. For example, the term *bug* is often used by computer types in reference to hardware software errors (e.g., "I have a bug in my program that I can't find"). This term has its mythological origin in a story in which computer pioneer Admiral Grace Hopper reportedly found a real bug to be the cause of a malfunction in an early mainframe computer.

Juniors and seniors use more sophisticated cues to supplement terminology.

> Maybe their body language, a little bit. If they're frustrated, you can tell they're not going to be easy to work with. (senior)

Tip-offs [for students who don't know what they're doing] were body language. Helpless. Dumbfounded. They would back away and their hands would go up and just . . . they're not sitting there digging in. . . . (senior)

Nonmajors in introductory computer classes are often so highly stressed that even fan and keyboard noises threaten to push them over the edge. They come to the lab to get work done; they work quietly and can't wait to leave when they are finished. A sacred ambiance reminds one of a library or a church; talking, when it occurs, is hushed. It is obvious that the computer majors own the Micro lab. They aren't there just to get work done. It is both a home and a professional club. CIS majors move around more and are more animated. Like priests in churches and librarians in libraries, majors in labs talk louder and more often. They are at home in the labs and act as though they belong there.

Most students are using word processing programs. A few are using the Internet network to look up information. A few others are playing Solitaire and Minefield. The interesting thing is they sit here quietly. One CIS major talks with everyone in a wide radius around her. When she wasn't successful in engaging anyone in a conversation, she began talking to another CIS major at a computer table across from her. She is oblivious to the fact that she might be bothering others. The two of them talk a bit, her loudly, him softly. She is a graduating senior; he is a freshman. Will he learn to talk loudly too? (Rigoni, from field notes)

As I was observing students in the labs, I noticed that majors even seem to type at their keyboards differently. They are more casual about it, resting their hands on the keyboard base and reaching comfortably for keys. Fingers glide over keyboards like bluegrass guitarists touching strings, barely moving, wasting no energy. Their hands linger; they know their instruments. Other students attack keys deliberately, their fingers striking and recoiling, afraid to make mistakes.

I see two students helping others. One is a nonmajor helping a friend. They are using an Internet browser; something they are reading is obviously amusing to both of them. The other student has a different "air" about him. He is helping a student sitting at a specialty computer attached to a graphics scanner. He is instructing her to "try this" and when that doesn't work, "try this." He talks in his normal voice, loud by lab standards. It is distracting in an environment where the only other noise is from keyboards. Whatever they are attempting doesn't work. He shrugs his shoulders, says "Oh well," and walks away; it is obviously her problem and he isn't going to spend much time dealing with it. (Rigoni, from field notes)

CIS majors are in great demand in the lab. Everyone knows them; everyone has a question. Majors on duty as lab assistants will help a student until a problem is solved. Off-duty majors will help briefly, politely, trying the obvious solutions, but if the problem is more complex, it is someone else's problem—the student will have to figure it out or ask a lab assistant. Although this might seem callous, it is largely a matter of survival. Desperate, hopeful eyes of ordinary students follow majors as they enter the lab, and the ordinary students immediately ask for help. If majors are to get their own work done, they learn to say "no." A major told me she sometimes felt like Jesus in the musical *Jesus Christ Superstar*, when the mass of humanity wanting to be healed were all reaching out to him until he shouted, "No more!"

Another CIS major is in the hallway. He is obviously someone "in the know." He walks out into the common hallway and talks loudly to a young woman about his classes. He comes into the lab two more times to answer other questions for students who have sought his help in the hallway. He never stays very long. He answers the question, then leaves quickly. He returns to the hallway and talks loudly to the lab assistant on duty. He is obviously a member of the club. I hear him say good-bye to the LA [lab assistant]. (Rigoni, from field notes)

The ability to perform magic that others cannot duplicate on these machines helps form a personal persona. The demands by other students are part of the ritual. The decision about whether and how much to help is another part. In exchange for their expertise, CIS students are paid a certain homage, an introduction to the kind of respect they hope to experience as computer "professionals."

A CIS major sits down at a specialty computer. He uses a desktop publishing program. He talks for a while in a normal voice to a friend near him. Different students stop and talk to him and ask him questions. Courtesy?

Homage? He smiles and nods. The waves caused by his arrival subside. He gets down to work. (Rigoni, from field notes)

Computer majors divide those they are helping into two groups: those who care and those who don't care. Majors expressed a willingness to take the time to explain *how* to do a computer task to someone who showed an interest in learning it. In contrast, they would simply *do* the computer task for those they perceived as interested in the final product but disinterested in the intricacies of the task itself.

Basically, you just try and walk them through what you're doing and try and tell them what's wrong with the computer, and it would be important in the future to tell them how to fix it and what they can do. Otherwise just fix it; if they don't care, just fix it for them. (freshman)

I know basically everyone and what they're doing, I've seen them so many times that I know they're going to use Quattro Pro for accounting. They have to learn it. I'm going to show them how to use it right. But if it was a [Health Science] major, they don't care how it works anyway; they just want to get a chart out. I'll just show them the quickest way; in fact, I help them more and do most of the work for them to get the job done. (sophomore)

It is easier to just solve a problem for someone than to explain what the problem is and how to solve it and avoid it in the future. When someone doesn't care about how it is done, CIS majors take the easy route. It is a quick, ritual demonstration of expertise; I know how to do this, and I can help you. If someone is interested in the why behind a problem, majors expressed a willingness to take the time to help the student understand the problem and the solution. This is a more complex ritual demonstration of expertise; I know how to do this, and I can explain it to you if you care to peek into my world; I know a lot, but I'll simplify it so you can understand it. Professionalism is reinforced in either case.

I used to think faculty were the smartest people on the campus. When faculty come in, and they ask you questions or call you over to the phone and ask you how things work . . . it's stuck; I'm locked up; I can't do this; can you format a disk for me? When someone comes up and says can you format a disk for me, I know I'm smart. (sophomore)

This CIS student who worked as a lab assistant summarizes the value of the ritual activity in the lab. His words demonstrate the outcomes of the ritual activity. The lab work has afforded him the ability to use professional terminology and knowledge as if he were already a computer professional while binding him to his group and separating him from ordinary people (who happen to include faculty he used to view as smart). He is developing a view of himself as a professional who is smarter than others who he "used to think were the smartest people on campus."

*Transmission of Myth*

> Perhaps some of them might have found an answer to the first question, but that answer would have led them to other questions that would take them, slowly and most probably by degrees, into a weird world. A world that cannot be described but only hinted at, and that can only be discussed, if there would ever be any point in discussing it, with someone who has walked the same, or a very similar, road.
>
> Janwillem van de Wetering, *A Glimpse of Nothingness:*
> *Experiences in an American Zen Community*
> (New York: Washington Square Press, 1988), 63.

Myths are narrative forms of world view truths. They are stories that frame how an individual within a particular world view is expected to view reality and by extension is expected to act. Students in the latter stages of the CIS program are able to skillfully articulate the professional mythology handed down by faculty and other professionals with whom they come into contact.

> This transmission of meaning occurs not only in formal education, but also in the daily routines and in "the informal annotations of everyday experience we call common sense." [2]

Ritual and myth play crucial roles in the worldmaking activity of professional apprentices. The two intertwine and are separated primarily as points of emphasis, with ritual focusing on external activity and myth focusing on internal activity. They are essentially descriptions of the same elephant. The earlier description of the ritual binding and separation of majors in the lab can be legitimately viewed as the development of a professional mythic account of nonmajors that helps to define majors as a group. As might be expected, the depiction of nonmajors is primarily a negative definition. Nonmajors are like this; majors are not.

[non-computer majors] get frustrated easy. They don't understand. They try to skip steps in a sequence of things to do. . . . They just don't take things in steps, in certain orders. (sophomore)

[non-computer majors] don't listen and they don't pay attention to what they're doing. I might tell someone how to do it, but they don't think about what they're doing while they're doing it. I think a part of that too is they don't practice it enough. (sophomore)

Majors are indirectly defined here as people who don't get frustrated easily, do understand, do not skip steps in a sequence, listen, pay attention to what they are doing while they are doing it, and they practice enough. It is easy to see in these statements about nonmajors a developing perspective that will help form the professional identity obvious in late-program students and graduates. Underlying the lab rituals are cultural stories and myths that delimit the "tribe" of computer professionals from everyone else. Traweek's study of physicists shows how subtle this delimitation can be.

Deeper even than submerged assumptions about gender and national identity are profound and deeply felt tensions about time that I find coiled at the center of this culture. In the course of a career a physicist learns the insignificance of the past, the fear of having too little time in the present, and anxiety about obsolescence in the face of a too rapidly advancing future.[3]

Even among CIS students, students differentiated computer majors into two mythic groups: the strong and the weak. The exact terms *strong* and *weak* are not universally used by students; I have chosen to use these terms because they indicate both faculty and student appraisals of which students succeeded at the minimum preparation level and which students went beyond that minimum. A *weak* student is successful enough to graduate and receives a lukewarm recommendation; a *strong* graduate is the type of student who graduates with honors and receives an enthusiastic recommendation. It is interesting that strong majors were identified not so much by objective criteria such as technical competence but by more social criteria inherent in the silent curriculum such as work habits, initiative, and ability to function in groups. Traweek observed a similar phenomenon in the recommendations of physics graduate students.

> [Laudatory phrases in letters of recommendation suggest that] the ideal student is a "hard and willing worker," "careful, meticulous, and thorough," a "good colleague" who always "delivered" and had a good sense of what was possible.[4]

Stronger majors are defined by other students both by negative and positive definitions. As negatively defined, a strong major is not easily frustrated by the innumerable errors inherent in computer work and does not ask for help. As positively defined, a strong student is committed to the major, spends a great deal of time on computer tasks, does more than the minimum, and actually has fun working on computer tasks.

The willingness to invest a great deal of lab time is an important student myth throughout the program. Good students put in the time; weak students do what they must do and leave. This is an important construction transmitted early in the program.

> The better students will probably be in the lab more often, but they'll be more efficient with what they do, and the poorer students will be in the lab usually less, but they may take more time on a particular topic than somebody that's more proficient at it. (freshman)

It is of interest that a freshman is able to articulate the all-important time-spent criterion. This criterion is really two separated but related ones: 1) time spent absorbing the cultural apprenticeship, and 2) efficient use of time. Not only do strong students spend more time in the lab than weak students, they are more productive in the use of that time. The implication is that a good student will get a great deal more done in the lab than a weak student. This corresponds to Goffman's research, which shows that "the degree of involvement is the degree of commitment to a social encounter, and for each encounter there is an expected level of involvement."[5] A senior cites the trait of time commitment and adds the imperative to find solutions without asking for help. She cites the often-repeated cultural wisdom of finding other important information en route to finding the one answer that prompted the search.

> Those who succeed [are] willing to put in a lot of time until they get it right or until it takes them wherever they're going. I succeeded, and I know a couple of others who did. We have a tendency to not ask for help but to get out the manuals and dig through them and in a few hours find out what we needed to know, but we also got 30 other things on the way to finding out that specific bit of information. . . . Don't ask for help. After a couple of hours I have gone and asked for help, but very rarely. I'd rather find it out myself. (senior)

In addition to spending a lot of time in the lab and not asking for help, computer majors also are expected to enjoy what they do. Connected to not getting upset with errors they encounter, majors often use the word "play" to describe their time using the computer. Strong computer majors are expected to "play" and to "enjoy" the work they do. The problems they solve are puzzles, challenging situations they get the privilege to solve.

> The people that I have seen quit the major are the ones who go in and start working on the computer and don't seem to be really enjoying themselves. They're going through the motions. If they're not in there enjoying themselves, and saying when they get a program done, "Wow, it does this." They're in there; okay, I got it done, next one. They don't seem to have fun with it. . . . As you play on it, you learn. (junior)

Ultimately, It is by spending the lab time in productive play that a student demonstrates commitment to the major. This commitment to intense lab work appears to be a prerequisite for mastery of the silent curriculum. Perhaps the repetition of tasks and the solving of endless problems creates a bridge to the silent knowledge. By doing what they have been asked to do, by doing what they can do, students are rewarded with this deeper knowledge.

> You have to be committed to it. I see people thinking that they can goof off and not work . . . that might be true of any major. [Commitment means] just spending the time in the lab, on the computer, or looking at the book or understanding what's going on. (graduate)

[The attitude of weak students and students who don't succeed is] Get a grade; do it and pass. It's okay. Sometimes, I envy that. Admire that. That ability to relax . . . [They do] last-minute work. [They] start a project too late. Not taking time. Not interested in anything beyond what was absolutely required. They just wanted the information to fulfill the assignment and go do something else. (senior)

I saw some people really worried about the technical down to the nitty gritty stuff. Like a COBOL program that didn't work or something. I saw other people, like myself, that like to look at a little bit bigger view and didn't worry so much about that. If something wasn't working right, I was okay. For instance, some of them ask for help a lot more, where others want to try and figure things out for themselves or don't let it bother them so much. (graduate)

I think maybe some of the people that are less successful ask for help too soon. Whereas the more successful will beat their heads against the screen and try to find it on their own. They'll have, I don't know if patience is the right word, but they have more motivation to find it on their own. (senior)

A graduate indicates how the construction looks in its full development. It indicates on-the-job confirmation of its professional importance.

I think [those who didn't ask for help] learned more. I felt like I learned more because I tried to figure it out on my own, and now that I'm out working, I think that really helped me because you can't do that. There are people that you call and hot lines that you can call and that's great. You can do that, but if you don't have a good stab at it yourself, and you haven't tried the common things then you don't even know what to ask. (graduate)

## Student World View Reconstruction

But meanwhile we are to do the best we can. What task we may find, do it as well as you can. Let the general try to win his battle, the merchant to make his fortune, let the philosopher try to connect his theories and let the engineer invent and use. If the attempt meets with success the result is of no importance. A medal or a rotten tomato, the result is of no importance.

Janwillem van de Wetering, *A Glimpse of Nothingness:*
*Experiences in an American Zen Community*
(New York: Washington Square Press, 1975), 99.

The ritual activity and myth transmission work together to construct a comprehensive professional world view revolving around the main goals of the silent curriculum noted earlier in this chapter: the ability to adapt to rapid change, the ability to construct conceptual frames, and the ability to solve problems. Allied to these main goals are satellite elements such as spending enough time on a project and working through problems without seeking help.

Students begin to look to each other rather than to instructors for help. Professors emphasize that students need to learn to work on their own because in a very short time there will be no professors available to help them find their solutions. Students learn to successfully guide each other. This appears to be an important stage in the building of the professional identity.

We were left kind of on our own and that was good to an extent . . . in the extent of finishing the project and trying to solve the problems ourselves by talking with each other and with other group members, other members of a different team. Trying to help each other out. I think of being out in the work force, you're really not going to have a head person to go run to for help. (senior)

The reluctance to ask for help is a subset of the idea of "acting like a warrior." To ask for help without having given it your best is something that an "ordinary person" would do.

Students begin to verbalize some of the main goals of the silent curriculum and occasionally echo the voices of their professors. One student said:

The main thing I've learned is that you don't learn any of these programs. You don't learn programming, you learn concepts in how to learn programming and how to learn new programs because everything's changing so fast, there's no way you can keep up with it unless you learn how to learn. (junior)

A senior expresses the constant change noted by the junior and frames the computer as a tool for problem solving rather than its centerpiece. His comments also document the development of his professional identity over the four years of the program.

I guess when it comes right down to it, probably more than anything, [I have learned] to solve problems; and it's not really the computer, it's everything.

I guess it relates back to how I look at things in more detail than I ever would have in the past. That probably more than anything. I originally thought coming into the major, they taught you how to do everything with the little computer and you're off. You'll learn this—next month will be different; you're going to have to learn it over. They taught me a way to learn new things and to solve the problems that I didn't understand. (senior)

Indeed, problem solving stands as the key element of the new world view. The most glaring difference between *strong* and *weak* students involves their world view on problem solving. Although these terms are concrete expressions of student competence, they are, in fact, subtle judgments resulting from student interaction in classes, in labs, and in group work. In classes, students judge other students based on cues from professors. When a professor offers a student's solution to a problem as being particularly "elegant," other students know that person did a good job. Faculty and students pay attention to where students sit in class, how much they contribute, and the kinds of questions they ask. In lab work, students' abilities to do their work with a minimum of effort and to grasp and use the more esoteric aspects of an assignment favorably affect judgments. A student who can successfully help another student solve a problem is sometimes regarded as a national treasure. Success in group work involves students working well in groups and contributing without dominating.

Strong students achieve the goals of the silent curriculum; they identify with the goals and processes of that curriculum. Strong students better match the views of the faculty than weak students. Essentially, the faculty provide cues as to who is strong or weak by establishing the prevailing mythology. Some, but not all, weak students drop out of the program by their junior year. But as with most programs, some of the weak students perform at a minimal level and do well enough to graduate.

CIS faculty clearly establish the most important items in the silent curriculum.

I think problem solving is inherent in being able to write a computer program. It's also inherent in the whole heart of designing a computer system. Problem solving is just inherent in the field. (Dr. A)

[The three important curriculum components are] business knowledge, computer skill, communication skill . . . and problem solving is the very key ingredient and link between all these other three. Problem solving has got to be essential to this whole thing. (Dr. B)

One faculty member, after describing his problem-solving technique as based on "fasting and prayer," goes on to describe the development of a checklist approach to computer problem solving.

> I don't know how to describe it, it's sort of like going down the mental checklist. At this stage I have run into so many problems over such a long period of time, it's sort of like—what happened before? I may not be able to place the event or the circumstance where a similar problem arose, but it's going down the list. Could it be this? Could it be this? It's like Star Trek.
> "Mr. Spock, can you locate the source of the transmissions."
> "No Captain, the sensors can't do that."
> "Can you locate where the source is or not."
> We do it by process of elimination, and you just go down until you get lucky. You hit something that seems to allow you to make progress. (Dr. C)

To a freshman, the emphasis in problem solving appears to fall largely on defining the problem itself and making an educated guess. This appears to begin the process of building a repertoire of problem solutions from which to choose. At this point, a problem is still an objective fact, an obvious, tangible reality that needs to be fixed.

> The first thing is to find out where the problem is and the importance of the problem. Once you determine where the problem is to think about how you can solve that problem . . . you go on to try things, educated guesses a lot of times. You just see what happens. If you plug or unplug something, it could cause reactions based on what's happening and what you do. I think one of the major differences [with poor problem solvers] is that they don't know what the problem is exactly. I think that's a big key in solving the problem is knowing where the problem is. (freshman)

A number of things are of particular interest in this student's account. One is the accurate perception that the most important part of problem solving is knowing "what the problem is exactly." Although this is accurate, this freshman version of this truth is limited. It still views problems in terms of technical problems that can be solved by plugging or unplugging something. Also, although he accurately reiterates his professor's notion of educated guesses, the notion of an ordered checklist from which these guesses are drawn is largely absent. It is there in a primitive state, but it is yet too vague a concept to articulate. Traweek indicates that physicists are trained in a similar manner; she even echoes the computer student's use of the word *plug*.

> Students are given "problem sets" to solve in order to demonstrate their comprehension of the material. In "easy" problems, the students merely "plug" data into the appropriate mathematical formulae. Harder problems require the students either to recognize data in an unfamiliar form and see that it can be analyzed in ways that have already been learned, or to pick out which known formulae will serve to analyze data which are perhaps deceptively familiar.[6]

Sophomores and juniors continue to build their problem-solving checklists. Solutions are viewed less as educated (almost randomly lucky) guesses and more as a process resulting from a knowledge and experience base. Sophomores still view problems and their solutions almost exclusively as application or programming problems rather than organizational problems; answers to tough problems can be still be found in textbooks.

> First, I try to relate to something I've done before. . . . The first thing I do is I think, have I done something like this before, and if I have and something is similar, then I'll use that same transition. I'll say, okay, I must have to do it this way. If I absolutely can't figure it out . . . then I'll go and get a book. I know basically how to read a computer book now, too, where to find the information quick, and I can look at it and know right away how it works. (sophomore)

By contrast, advanced programmers begin to see solutions as modular, with smaller, local solutions building into larger, global solutions.

> First, I pick it [a problem] apart. I dissect it into its individual systems. I know what the whole looks like; now I want to identify it into its parts. Then I look at how each part works. You can't solve a problem until you know how it works. It's like the body—all the parts are interrelated. If something doesn't work, I subdivide that part into smaller parts until I get it to work. (junior)

This reflects a fundamental step important in programming solutions to problems. This process appears to be a result of having built a large enough repertoire of solved problems. Once solved, a problem is no longer a problem; it is part of a solution. Again, Traweek found similarities in studying physicists.

> Teachers show [physics] students how to recognize that a new problem is like this or that familiar problem; in this introduction to the repertoire of soluble problems to be memorized, the student is taught not induction or deduction but analogic thinking.[7]

One professor expressed the view that students learn an incredible amount in every class; the problem they face, he says, is that everything is always new. It isn't until they reach a point at which everything is not new that students begin to understand how much they have learned.

A junior who had not yet taken the systems analysis sequence illustrated the sophisticated approach he used to problem solve in programming applications. After learning the basics of programming, he said, "It becomes more complex, but it doesn't become any harder." He accurately perceives that *difficulty* and *complexity* are separate problem-solving properties and that complexity does not imply difficulty. Like most computer students, this junior learned to develop problem-solving solutions using a process called "flow charting"; this process utilizes one-dimensional shapes such as circles, rectangles, and diamonds to designate different program actions. He developed his own way of visualizing his solutions that reflects definite sophistication.

> I'd always visualize it three-dimensionally . . . it wasn't just a rectangle but more cubical, and circles would become spheres. I never just viewed it linearly cause it's too restricting. In programming, you're taught to go top-down, but I never did that. I program in three dimensions all over the place and later tailor it to a top-down approach. I could have things going all over the place, and then, suddenly, something would feel right, and I'd go with it. I think programming is an art and I think you have to go with how it feels rather than how you think it should go. You know how you have to do it for yourself, but then for optimal success you have to give the end user what they want. (junior)

The fact that this student uses three-dimensional models is less important than the fact that he has developed a personal model for handling the complexities involved. Programming is not a drab, mechanical exercise for him. It is, rather, an art form, and his art involves nonlinear creations that are later tailored to fit the linear requirements. Not simply a logical process, this view introduces the notion that a solution has a style and a feel. He has made a clear personal investment in the profession.

Though successful seniors can also continue with this program-oriented problem/solution approach, their expressions depict a tendency toward more global viewpoints than sophomores and juniors. They are better able to verbalize the silent curriculum. Some students begin to perceive problem solving as something not necessarily connected to programming. One senior demonstrates particular fluency in describing the official problem-solving approach.

> [I go] back to what I've actually been taught; it works. What I do is look at what I need to end up with. What do I need to start with and what happens in the middle to get messed up between what I want in the end and where I started? Am I missing some start point, or did something go wrong in the middle? I usually start at the end, go to the beginning, and if the beginning is all clear, go to the middle. (senior)

Eventually, the ultimate question, "Why is there a problem?" is asked. It announces yet another level of sophistication in problem solving, a recognition that the word *problem* is itself a construction. If a situation has existed for some time, what event or condition suddenly turned it into a problem? Two seniors expressed it like this:

> I like to open up books and look . . . for anything similar to the problem. Anything related in any way, any little bits of information that can help me. [I look at] what the outcome should be. What's needed to solve the problem? What information do you have in the beginning? Why is there a problem? (senior)

> I examine things a lot more than I ever did in the past. I want to know why something is wrong or why there's a problem. I look at it in so much more

detail. I probably do it with more than just problems. I look at everything in more detail than I ever would have in the past. I pick things up that I guess my friends are amazed at. (senior)

These approaches contrast dramatically with a problem-solving approach by a senior who was thought of as weak by the faculty and students alike.

I want to solve it [a problem] as soon as possible. Even if I don't come to the right conclusion. But if it's serious I probably want to wait. Cause I have trouble making decisions. (senior)

This response is the antithesis of good problem solving. First, the desire to solve the problem "as soon as possible" is itself problematic. A maxim from computer folklore states that for an accurate indication of how long a job should take, you should decide how much time a project should take, double it, and move it to the next highest time increment. For example, if I think I should be able to complete a project in two hours, I multiply that times two (four hours) and move it to the next time increment. The project will likely take me four days. This is only a slight exaggeration. Computer majors are taught early: plan enough time, this will take you a lot longer than you think. Second, a willingness to arrive at a solution "even if I don't come to the right conclusion" is the closest thing to the concept of sin—a violation of "professional" morality—possible to a computer professional. This view simply would not be accepted by a real professional; if a solution doesn't work, it requires more time and more work. Period.

The most complete view of computer problem solving comes from successful graduates working as computer professionals. The perspective adopts an organizational context in which programming has faded totally into the background. This problem-solving approach includes asking whether or not something is really a problem, and, if it is, whom it affects and how critical it is. It also assumes that a problem may have more than one possible solution.

If there's a problem, first of all, I need to find out what's the problem, or if it is really a problem. I need to find out who it's affecting. Is it affecting one person? How critical is it to this one person? Really, I need to talk to the person to make sure what they say is the problem is really the problem. What's the benefits [*sic*] of solving the problem versus can it wait, what's the time criticalness of this. Of course then find your solutions, analyze which one is good, and after you put the solution in affect [*sic*], follow up, see if it worked. If it didn't work, you need to do something else. I guess that's about it. I guess my biggest problem-solving skill is you just don't jump right in and think that you have a solution. There could be so many consequences, you don't just jump in and put your first thought into it. If doesn't work, you're really in trouble. (graduate)

This description indicates a multifaceted approach with a series of checkpoints. The problem itself is checked and rechecked; how serious is the problem; how many people does it affect? The approach is cautious and purposeful. Once a problem is defined, multiple solutions are examined and a good one is chosen. Results are checked; does the solution meet the client's expectations? There is no hurry. Unlike the poor problem solver described earlier, this one feels, "my biggest problem-solving skill is you just don't jump right in and think that you have a solution." She is a classic computer problem solver.

## Loss and Renewal

> He looks quiet and pleasant. There is only a little old man who wants to point out something to you. Nothing will remain. You will lose your name, your body, and your character. Your fear diminishes.
>
> Janwillem van de Wetering, *A Glimpse of Nothingness:*
> *Experiences in an American Zen Community*
> (New York: Washington Square Press, 1975), 35–36.

Don Juan emphasizes to Carlos Castaneda that, in terms of how "ordinary" individuals would view it, becoming a sorcerer entails great loss. Becoming a sorcerer means leaving behind the "ordinary" reality; for all that is gained, there is also loss. Schön states that part of the process of differentiation includes a potential for actual loss. Facing potential loss of everything they already know and value, apprentices sometimes find the costs of gaining professional mastery greater than the rewards.

Younger CIS majors whose social roles are still very flexible seem to intuitively grasp the issue of loss; older majors who have more established social roles often have personally experienced such loss. Younger, traditional students, both male and female, generally feel that they are, as computer majors, viewed as intelligent and hardworking. Yet they are often concerned about the negative cultural association attributed to technological experts, such as being perceived as "introverted" and "nerdy." This gives them a genuine ambivalence about their major. Interestingly, none of the students whom faculty thought of as the "top" students expressed this ambivalence. There might be reason to suspect that those who did not wish to be fully identified as computer majors were prevented by lack of a social role commitment from being as successful as they might have been.

Several male students expressed the fear of being perceived as too brainy or too "geeky."

There's certain people that I say that I'm going into computers, and there's certain people that I just say, "Well I'm not sure yet." If I know them from high school, and I want them to think of me as a real bright person, I'll say that I'm going into computers. Usually if it's someone that I played hockey with in high school, I tell them that I'm just taking generals yet . . . probably because I don't want them to think of me as the brain or something. I don't want to be stereotyped at this point, I guess. (sophomore)

A student with a dual major in CIS and International Management, although a successful computer major, expresses a particular ambivalence.

Computer majors, at least to me, don't seem to mingle as much as say a business major or nursing or something like that. They're more on one side of the building, down in the labs working, but that's not all. I think at times they get a bad rap. It's kind of like what's your major? Computers [mumbles, holding hand over mouth]. I have to admit now, I say International Management before I say CIS. I would have to say the way I perceive it, I guess, I think of the geek, the person who doesn't have a social life, who doesn't really do that much, who has fun sitting down with a box. (senior)

Even one of the junior faculty members expressed concern about being stereotyped as a computer person.

I fit all the stereotypes. I look the part. . . . A tall, thin, young, white guy with thick glasses and generally a short haircut and pretty intense, and it's like you can see him coming a mile away. (Dr. C)

One student decided to turn an English minor into a major after completing the requirements for the computer major. The social role dynamics seemed to have considerable impact on this situation. She haltingly expressed her fears of being identified negatively as a computer major; yet, after graduation, she intends to find employment as a computer professional.

> Yeah . . . I guess I was telling myself . . . well, the stereotypical computer person, it's like I don't want to be that, you know, with the glasses . . . so I kind of had a negative view of [the major] . . . and I still do to a certain extent.
> Well . . . uhmm . . . most [English majors] didn't look like computer majors. (senior)

Two nontraditional students acknowledged significant social losses as a result of their world view transformation. One lost a close friend when her life took a different path as she moved from a "pink collar" to a professional occupation.

> When I came to college . . . I had a certain friend that kind of shied away from me and still kind of shies away from me, no matter what I've done. It's to say that just because now I have a college degree, I'm not any better. I'm still the same person. . . . She was the type of person who always talked about going to nursing school but then she had a baby, got married, and then got divorced, then had another baby . . . it's just like her life never let her do that, or she never let herself do that because of her life. So I guess when I did it, I did feel like she really shied away from me. (graduate)

Another student paid a much greater price as her education changed fundamental views of what she wanted and expected from life, and as that changed her relationship with her family.

> I grew too much. I found my limits. I cracked. I survived it. I found myself. . . . I'm alone now. I'm not married. My husband's raising the kids. . . . I decided I deserved to do what I want in order to survive. I have to do and do and do in order to survive or I'll die. It just happened. I'd heard that women returning to school end up changing and getting a divorce. I vowed that it would never happen to me, but it did. (senior)

# SUMMARY

The explicit curriculum in this professional computer program focuses on computer application programs, programming languages, systems projects, and management courses. The implicit silent curriculum embraces change and adaptability; conceptual frames and visualization; and, most importantly, problem solving. The explicit curriculum *can* be learned directly; the silent curriculum *cannot*. Successful professional apprentices appear, during the early stages, to follow the time-honored shamanic practice of committing to the surface teachings while remaining essentially unaware of the deeper reality transformation caused by those teachings. The silent knowledge accrued gradually evolves into a new reality construction that is in many, perhaps most, situations as unexamined and reified as the construction it replaces. The principal means by which the professors have an affect on these changes in reality construction include assignments, language, culture, and modeling behavior. Considered collectively, they are subsumed by the Durkheimian approach to ritual and myth development.

The computer lab provides a setting for the basic ritual activities that influence computer reality constructions. Most assignments require the lab for all or part of their completion. It is in the lab that computer apprentices are able to demonstrate tasks that afford them respect and status. A whole range of computer major behaviors mark the lab as a "sacred" area in which students are knowledgeable and comfortable. Computer students appear to expect both deference and homage in this area. It is a place where ritualistic interaction occurs between computer apprentices; between apprentices and their professors; and between apprentices and "others." It is a place of physical interaction with the total society. It is here that apprentices build their problem solution toolboxes, separate themselves from nonmajors, and bind themselves to other apprentices.

For Durkheim, myth develops from ritual experiences. The computer lab interaction results in a mythology that defines the good and the poor classifications in relationship to students, questions, problem-solving techniques, and programming techniques. Juniors and seniors readily articulate the mythic curricular views acquired during their ritual performances. For computer students to be judged successful, they are expected to make a commitment to their studies that is demonstrated by several explicit and interconnected criteria. They begin to judge each other by the degree to which they adhere to this social criteria. First, they connect success with the investment of a great deal of time, especially lab time. They expect those who are successful to "play" with computers and to demonstrate a visible enjoyment of the time spent on curriculum tasks. They expect this sense of play to be demonstrated by always doing more than the minimum required for any task. Finally, students expect those who are successful to complete most tasks without asking for help from professors.

Examination of these criteria provides clear indications about the way basic problem-solving abilities are developed in this CIS program. If problem solving must be learned indirectly, students must actively participate in the surface ritual (assignments and lab behaviors) and build to a cumulative result through the repetition and expansion of these tasks. The students' criteria for success should not be surprising. This approach echoes the traditional advice of writing teachers to students who would be writers to "write, write, write." Any student who spends a great deal of time in activities requiring problem solving is going to experience more kinds of problems to solve.

Students who do more than is expected are going to face problems of greater complexity and difficulty and will experience the connectivity of the various problems and solutions. The more problems students encounter, the more solutions they will devise. The more mentally active students are, the more they will seek out problems and develop solutions. The solutions to little problems form a base that leads to solutions of larger, more complex problems. This all takes a large time commitment. Students who do not spend enough time learning to solve a large array of problems cannot develop the necessary skills. Poor students will have few skills; weak students will have limited skills; successful students will have extensive skills.

The requirement that a student must enjoy this time commitment serves a twofold purpose. First, a student is not likely to continue doing something that is distasteful. Mark Twain reminded us in *Tom Sawyer* that work is something we have to do and that we hope to do as little of as possible. Work is something we simply want to "get done"; we prefer to fill our time with as much play as possible. Second, the requirement that computer activity be treated as play provides the opportunity for viewing and handling problems differently. We work differently than we play. Play allows facile manipulation of perspectives; when we play we don't watch a clock or hurry to arrive at a premature solution. When we play, time passes very quickly and painlessly. Computer professionals speak incessantly about how quickly the time passed; this is because the tasks are really a form of play.

Finally, the not-asking-for-help criterion forces an individual student to problem solve. Problem solving is very personal. Help is helpful only when a student has done all the important preliminary work; otherwise the helper solves the problem, but the student cannot possibly understand why the solution worked. When that happens, nothing has occurred that is of any value to the student. It is interesting that students in this study were much more emphatic about the importance of not asking for help than the faculty were on the issue.

Even as ritual and myth construct a professional computer identity, other held identities are necessarily destroyed, marginalized, or merged to make room for the new construction. The resulting constructions may also provide mixed benefits. The same rituals and mythology that provide status in a lab setting may result in loss outside that sacred setting. As group membership becomes more defined, it requires the exiting of certain other roles. This often results in varying degrees of loss for students.

Students seem to instinctively understand that gain and loss are different sides of the same social coin. Although most of the computer students expressed a certain pride at being viewed as intelligent, some of them were less comfortable with the accompanying perception of being "nerds." There also seemed to be at least some correlation between success and fear of being labeled as a nerd. Interestingly, the males and females who most seemed to fear such a label from their nondepartmental friends were generally considered less successful by their teachers and their departmental peers. Though it is possible that they were simply perceived as being less successful because they limited their identification with the major, it seems likely that their reluctance to fully embrace the computer role changed their commitment to the explicit curriculum, which in turn altered their mastery of the silent curriculum. There seemed to be a definite correlation with those students who had problems identifying with the major and those who struggled with the programming languages. Although correlation does not imply cause and effect, the difficulty with social role transition might help us to understand these students' struggles. These students did not seem secure enough in the new role to completely abandon the old.

Likewise, students in this study seem to build constructions resembling the silent curriculum. Freshmen develop a construction that frames their extensive work with application software as preparation for a career using this software; sophomores introduce the element of programming to this basic view. Upperclassmen develop more sophisticated frames that provide them with more realistic occupational prospects. These outlooks, which focus on systems analysis and design, communication and group skills, and problem solving, increasingly illustrate the goals of the silent curriculum.

Silent knowledge and its development have been explored as instrumental in the education of computer professionals. Does this mean that everything taught in the explicit curriculum serves no use? To the contrary, it is the explicit curriculum that serves as a doorway to the silent curriculum. Something that cannot be taught directly must be taught indirectly. The sequence of application packages, programming, and systems analysis and design seems to move students through successive temporary world views, and those world views obviously continue to grow on the job after graduation.

Highlighting the existence of a silent curriculum provides an opportunity for those involved in the explicit curriculum to examine it in a different context, to consciously reconstruct opportunities for indirect learning that might be impossible if one is not aware of its existence and function. It provides an opportunity to consciously construct what is presently done unconsciously. Bringing the silent curriculum to consciousness also provides an opportunity to reexamine the plight of students who are less successful in the explicit curriculum. Faculty might consider the plight of students caught in a social role bound by the demands of the silent knowledge they are attempting to accept. Strategies might be devised to make that conflict obvious so students can make conscious decisions that now remain unconscious. Faculty might be able to adjust the sequencing of class tasks and provide (and even require) more opportunities for practice to those who need it. Faculty might need to openly discuss how the explicit curriculum leads to indirect changes in the silent curriculum.

In short, examination of the silent curriculum provides opportunities for those of us who are engaged in education to reexamine our practice. It is an opportunity to become more of a master shaman. Viewing professional education from the perspective of shamanism does not imply that education is innately mystical. A shaman/teacher, to the contrary, is a very skillful, purposeful teacher whose world view leaves nothing to chance.

## NOTES

1. Philip Manning, *Erving Goffman and Modern Sociology* (Stanford, Calif.: Stanford University Press, 1992), 133.

2. Sharon Traweek, *Beamtimes and Lifetimes: The World of High Energy Physicists* (Cambridge: Harvard University Press, 1988), 74.

3. Traweek, *Beamtimes*, 17.

4. Traweek, *Beamtimes*, 83.

5. Manning, *Goffman*, 129.

6. Traweek, *Beamtimes*, 76.

7. Traweek, *Beamtimes*, 77.

# Chapter Six

# Insight and Resistance

It was impossible to get the Master to speak of God or of things divine. "About God," he said, "we can only know that we know nothing."

One day he told of a man who deliberated long and anxiously before embarking on discipleship. "He came to study under me, with the result that he learned nothing."

Only a few of the disciples understood: What the Master had to teach could not be learned. Nor taught. So all one could really learn from him was nothing.

Anthony de Mello, *One Minute Wisdom*
(New York: Doubleday, 1988), 173.

There are several widely quoted lines in T. S. Eliot's poem, *Four Quartets*, that state that at the end of our explorations, we find ourselves back at the point where we began and now truly know that place for the first time. This perfectly describes our current explorations. Having come full circle, we can now bring a new understanding to the situations and questions posed in the first chapter. I had asked why I initially didn't "get it" and then suddenly did, why some people "got it" and others didn't, and why Jodie wasn't able to understand the payroll problem algorithm. Let us reexamine these questions after arriving back at the beginning with a fresh perspective. Using the perspective of real education as world view alteration, some quite interesting points emerge.

First, from a student perspective: As it is the natural human inclination to maintain the status quo, altering one's world view requires time and risk investment. A student unconsciously decides how much to invest in terms of risk and time. Assuming a lack of secondary social constrictions (such as family obligations), investment may depend on how well a student has been "hooked" into the program. If the hook is not well placed, a student is likely to drop a particular program and find something else more appealing. In a sense, freshman students moving through a general curriculum are like fish in a pond asking to be hooked. When secondary social constrictions apply, a student may resist any hooks at all. Once a hook is set, the successful transformation of a student's world view will depend on how much time is spent immersed in the ritual and myth of that program.

Second, from an educator's perspective: The task of an educator is to create learning experiences. In truth, nothing at all can be taught. The total power of the teaching/learning experience rests in the hands of the learner. A teacher cannot force a learner to learn, yet a good learner can learn even from a poor teacher. The only thing teachers can do is to create rich learning experiences that facilitate a student's learning. We can create shortcuts for learners that can help them learn things more quickly and easily. Creating such learning experiences sometimes involves deception and trickery.

This last statement may cause some to recoil because, as a society, we don't like to think of teaching in these terms. Remember that these are shamanic terms. Perhaps it will be more palatable if I say that the creation of learning experiences involves enticement and invitation. The key to understanding this point is that we really don't want to see the world differently; we are comfortable as we are, even on the issue of our discomfort. If education involves seeing the world differently, trickery is needed to entice us to release our present view and peek at the world through a new lens. This is precisely what a learning experience does. But at the end of that experience, we tend to park that new view and return to our old view. However, when this experience is repeated often enough, it is likely that one day we will fully grasp the new world view and relinquish our old view. This event is often accompanied by a sense of awakening and rebirth. I maintain that this is the way real education always works. The fact that we do not often recognize the process does not change it.

Powerful learning experiences always involve some type of ritual participation and myth transferal. Even when we have students "cover material" that we deem essential, that material often cloaks the even more essential ritual and myth of the unteachable silent curriculum. We believe students either "get" or "don't get" these things. In fact, students "get" or "don't get" it for a very short list of reasons. A student may not be willing to invest in this world view or may not be willing to put in the time required for repeated glimpses of this view. Or a teacher may not have set up enough learning experiences for a student to grasp the world view.

In the end, both student and teacher are at a disadvantage because neither is consciously aware of the important processes. Teachers think they are teaching things, and students believe they are learning things. Teachers, as Schön points out, find it difficult to put words to what they know. Students, as Schön points out, are bewildered by trying to do what they simply do not understand. Hopefully, educators can become more conscious of this unconscious process that haphazardly works for some students and not others.

## WHY SOME "GET IT" AND SOME DO NOT

It is possible at this point to apply a new perspective to the question of why some professional students are successful while others are not. Students approach both the explicit and the silent curriculums with uneven backgrounds. If we consider the explicit curriculum as a means of developing the skills and perspectives required to change the world view of the students, those who arrive with more of those skills and perspectives will have an advantage.

I once read an interesting method of solving a type of complex word problem. Excitedly, I rushed into the office of a colleague and asked him to solve a sample problem. My intention was to impress him with this fascinating technique after he gave me the incorrect answer. To my surprise, he very quickly arrived at the correct solution. Disappointed by his quick solution, I asked him how he solved the problem. He proceeded to explain the very process I had just discovered. I left his office with the realization that somewhere in his life, he had encountered a similar problem, laid out a strategy for reaching a solution, and found that strategy efficient and helpful. Some of us encounter problems and develop strategies that never work, some develop inefficient strategies that nevertheless work, and others of us develop efficient strategies. We tend to cling to techniques that work even if they prove terribly inefficient.

A student who arrives in any program with a good grasp of the requisite skills for that program will have any easier time being successful, whether that program is computer science or English. However, the advantage one might have in one program will not necessarily transfer into an advantage in another. For example, my own success with the silent curriculum of an English major did not provide me with any apparent advantage as a computer major. Beyond the problem of not being able to speak the language of my professors, I had to build a base of silent knowledge to reach the starting point of many others in the program. Many women who attempt to enter the bastions of "male" science without the requisite science and math background encounter the same difficulty. Besides the inherent gender problems in the explicit curriculum, there is the problem of developing the requisite knowledge of the silent curriculum.

There seems to be a solution available to those who are persistent. Time spent on task appears to be a major criterion upon which success depends. If a student were to realize that the problem is often simply one of "catching up" to others, the problem is transformed into a time problem. It takes those who did not start off with an advantage more time to be successful. I believe this is what happened to me, and I believe I have seen this happen to many others. This is a point at which the explicit curriculum can make adjustments.

I had begun my computer program with such a deficit. My two semesters of Shakespeare and my semester of John Milton did not prepare me for the octal code dumps of mainframe assembly language. They did not prepare me to converse with Dr. Irving using math/computer terminology. They did not prepare me for sequential logic of computer algorithms. In short, they did not prepare me to think like a computer scientist. But other things were at work. I had been hooked well enough that I wasn't prepared to drop out of the program, and all the time I had spent in the computer lab working on assembly language programs provided enough ritual and myth to saturate my consciousness and cause me to dream about programming while I slept. So it simply took more time.

Students in my problematic problem-solving class were in various stages of preparation. It is never easy to definitively explain why individuals are less than successful, and it is important to note that explanation is not blame. For my part, I have no doubt I failed to hook some students and failed to provide others with enough of the silent curriculum to begin their transformation. For the students' part, I have no doubt some had social constrictions that prevented their buy-in. Some had time constraints that prevented their practice and in some cases prevented their catching up. Some may have decided they simply weren't interested.

Jodie certainly had social constrictions. She had the social and financial problems associated with being a single teenage parent. It is reasonable to assume she was busy making other significant world view adjustments and didn't have the luxury of working on this one. It is equally reasonable to assume she simply did not have the time to spend trying to solve problems she didn't understand. It seems likely that her social context worked against her in this class. I talked with her recently and found out that she had dropped out of school for a while, "straightened out" several of the problems in her life, and reentered school. She eventually graduated with a psychology major. She admits that the demands of teen parenthood made it difficult to spend enough time on the class assignments. She barely had enough time to *do* assignments, much less *play* with them. Her commitment to other social realities prevented her from committing to a new world view. Lack of commitment to a program is a difficult one for professors to accommodate. Although a teacher might be sympathetic and understanding about it, it is a barrier that prevents students from learning what is necessary to succeed. It appears that I couldn't help Jodie and the others like her in this class because I wasn't able to ask the right questions at the time.

# SO . . .

Although the viewpoints presented in this book appear to offer prospective, with great promise in helping to understand the educational process, I expect them to meet with the same types of resistance teachers encounter when trying to change students' world views. Individual human beings alter their world views only reluctantly. Groups of human beings seem to alter their world views even more reluctantly. This is especially true when the target view involves education. The contemporary education scene is crowded with dangerous crosswinds and undercurrents. Because everyone has gone to school, everyone feels like an expert on education. And today, most people use those views to advance political agendas and economic self-interests. This means that a very different way of looking at the educational process is going to encounter many different types of resistance. Just as individuals have significant personal investment in a status quo world view, social groups and institutions have even more political and financial investment and therefore more reasons to fiercely defend the status quo, even while talking incessantly about the need for systemic change. As thorough coverage of the resistance to education change would require a separate book on the subject, these pages will merely highlight some of the more obvious sources of resistance.

## WHY THE SILENT CURRICULUM IS IGNORED

After the Master attained Enlightenment, he took to living simply— because he found simple living to his taste.

He laughed at his disciples when they took to simple living in imitation of him.

"Of what use is it to copy my behavior," he would say, "without my motivation? Or to adopt my motivation without the vision that produced it?"

They understood him better when he said, "Does a goat become a rabbi because it grows a beard?"

Anthony de Mello, *One Minute Wisdom*
(New York: Doubleday, 1988), 67.

Several political forces from within the educational organization's world view make it difficult for teachers to advocate on behalf of a silent curriculum viewpoint. These forces revolve around issues outlined in earlier chapters. The forces include such things as a political division and subdivision of knowledge into turf-guarding academic departments and courses; a hierarchical placement of theory over practice; an archaic focus on the teacher rather than the learner, and a corollary view of teaching as the dispensing of knowledge rather than as the creating of learning experiences.

Dewey's list of features implies a corresponding list of resistances. The schools' prevailing assumptions about knowledge, the political division of knowledge into departments and courses, the priority given to teaching over coaching, and the prevailing conception of normal science research—all militate against acceptance of the conditions essential to creation of a research base appropriate to a reflective practicum.[1]

Other more subtle constraints exist as well. Goffman maintains that adults are constrained to avoid social roles for which they are unsuited. Individuals are not allowed to admit even to themselves anything "which the flow of events is likely to discredit."[2] This has implications in attempting to transmit something as invisible and indirect as a silent curriculum. This social constraint causes teachers to attribute students' silent curriculum failures to factors beyond their control, usually some flaw in the students' basic abilities or work habits. This view implies that certainly nothing more could be expected from the teacher, as the student is essentially flawed. The same constraint causes students to attribute their failure to something beyond their control, usually some flaw in the teacher or the program design. This view implies that certainly students cannot be expected to satisfy a teacher or a course's obscure and confusing demands. It attributes blame (our culture requires that blame be assigned to failure) to poor teaching. Even when students do learn the important lessons of the silent curriculum, teachers are seldom afforded much credit. Students see no evidence that teachers have had any significant role in their success, which they view as disconnected from the "hoops" of their classroom work. The myth emerges that a professional school is an "ivory tower" and the important things are learned only in "the real world." By engaging in face-saving activity, both teachers and students anticipate being labeled as failures but sidestep the effects of this label by attributing failure and blame to the other.

It is no wonder, then, that the explicit curriculum is the focus of educators. The more visible and direct explicit curriculum is, the easier it is for teachers to teach and for student to learn; by extension, it entails less risk for both parties. Students are better able to succeed with assigned explicit learning tasks; educators are easier able to prove success at the teaching tasks for which they are typically evaluated. The silent curriculum places more difficult demands on both teachers and students, but it places special pressure on the teachers. Goffman points out that social role failure hits unevenly on the mature members of society.

Younger students have greater license to fail without consequence; teachers, however, are increasingly at the mercy of disgruntled students, parents, administrators, and politicians (local, state, and national). Teachers, therefore, have an even greater incentive to "play it safe" by emphasizing the explicit curriculum and, by extension, those tasks with which students will be better able to "succeed" and save face. The role of an explicit curriculum, then, is to teach those explicit things that students can explicitly learn well enough to explicitly demonstrate them on a standardized test.

This is part of a lingering belief that all students really need is information. If only the correct information is made available to students, all other less visible facets of education will fall neatly into place. This viewpoint is apparent in teacher preparation programs in which content area departments consistently assert that the problem with public school teachers is that they don't have enough content area coursework. The idea seems to be that, though a little pedagogy won't harm preservice teachers, it is the content area information that will make them successful. The problem is that this is simply incorrect. While we have seen vast sums of money spent on educational campaigns to provide people with considerable information about the dangers of smoking, drugs, and unprotected sex, we have witnessed negligible changes in the behaviors targeted by those campaigns. Likewise, the new emphasis on content outcomes will better prepare preservice teachers to take high-stakes tests; it will not make them better at what they do.

In the case study outlined in this book, CIS program faculty openly admit that much of the content students learn within the official curriculum will certainly be outdated by the time students graduate. This is true despite the fact that the faculty work fervently to maintain a "cutting edge" curriculum. Yet, the things intended to be learned within the implicit silent curriculum will remain relevant throughout a graduate's professional career. The frustrating part of this to faculty and students alike is that the official curriculum is easier to teach and learn than the more important silent curriculum. In fact, the explicit curriculum is simply a means to accomplish this important learning. Yet, the teaching and learning of this silent curriculum is haphazard and unintentional. Professors and students alike hope that by carrying out the tasks of the official curriculum, students will pick up the subtle lessons well enough become successful professionals. The unintentional ritual of university education makes it unlikely that most students will escape without the accidental acquisition of at least some aspects of the silent curriculum, but it has not been consciously and purposefully utilized. If the silent curriculum is the essential core of an education, why is so little conscious attention given to it?

There are a number of reasons. First, as suggested earlier, the silent curriculum is fundamentally invisible; Schön demonstrates that even competent practitioners are essentially unaware of the assumptions that guide their practice. A society steeped in scientific principles has difficulty acknowledging and dealing with elements that are invisible. Second, aspects of the silent curriculum are haphazardly transmitted through the explicit curriculum. This creates an illusion that the explicit curriculum itself is changing students. In actuality, a process of natural selection seems to occur. Those students whose natural abilities developed in a particular direction and those students who are able to decipher the subtle cues are the only ones who grasp the silent curriculum and are successful. Other students are simply written off, as neither the teachers nor the students understand why they were unsuccessful. Each simply blames the other for their inadequacies. Third, the element of social risk outlined above becomes relevant. Because neither of the parties understands the real issues with which they are dealing, teachers categorize students as "not having it," and students voluntarily drop out of programs because they decided that "they really wanted to do something else." Both options help individuals to avoid the taint of failure.

The explicit curriculum is the gateway to the implicit silent curriculum. What is gained by recognizing this curricular relationship? Recognition works to make the invisible visible. Attending to the assumptions that underlie knowledge in general and professional practice in particular adds to a more thorough understanding of both. This is a necessary step in helping the explicit curriculum effectively work to the ends of the silent curriculum. It is a step that will help all students to have an equal opportunity to be successful and to accurately assess the role of a teacher. It is a step that will help teachers to reflect upon the complexity and subtlety of their understanding and the frustration their students experience on the path to their own silent knowledge.

## INTERLUDE: SHAMAN UNIVERSITY FANTASY

If shamans were trained in a contemporary setting . . .

Setting: An alternate reality much, much too close for comfort.
Scene: Shaman University: a for-profit school run by the Education-R-Us Group.

Camera opens on a large yellow banner with black letters containing the university slogan. It says, "An Education You Can Feel Good About." The scene fades and reopens on the evening class of Dr. Donald Juan, Shaman-in-Residence.

**Juan:** Mr. Strauss, thank you for being here after missing the past five weeks of class.

**Strauss** (Levi Strauss is a young man in his early twenties): I was working.

**Juan:** I need to remind you that attendance is a required part of this class.

**Strauss:** Look, Don. If I don't work, I can't afford to go to school. And besides, I'm not paying money to go to school here so you can treat me this way.

**Juan:** I don't suppose, Mr. Strauss, that you can see the irony in your argument.

**Strauss:** Huh?

**Juan:** I didn't think so. Try to get here, okay?

**Strauss:** Yeah, whatever.

**Juan:** Remember, this Saturday is your first lab. In order to help you secure a spirit-helper, we're going to bury you up to your neck in the school anthill.

**Castaneda** (Carla Castaneda is a thirty-something adult returning to school): Don, I chose this school because they told me I wouldn't need to do the anthill thing here. With all the money I'm paying to go here, I'm not going to do the anthill thing.

**Juan:** Ms. Castaneda, do you remember who told you that?

**Castaneda:** It was someone. I can't remember, Don.

**Juan:** Well Ms. Castaneda, I'm sorry someone told you that, but it is a very important part of the shaman experience, and it is required for this course.

**Castaneda:** This makes me very angry. This place is supposed to be flexible. I should have enrolled in Sorcerer State like I was first going to do. I'm NOT doing the anthill thing!

**Juan:** Okay, I can be flexible. Jivaro shamans drink *ayahuasca* to accomplish the same thing. We could do that instead.

**Castaneda:** I heard it tastes terrible. No way I'm drinking that stuff.

**Juan** (exasperated): So what do you want to do, just read a book about it?

**Castaneda:** A whole book? Hey, I work full-time, and I have a family to take care of. I don't have time to read a *book*.

**Juan:** Well, how about an article? Read an article about it and write a report on it.

**Castaneda:** I'll read the article, but no report. Man . . . I can't believe this place advertises itself as flexible.

**Strauss** (To Don Juan): You aren't going to get very good evaluations at the end of this course, you know.

Juan sits down at the desk in the front of the room. He quickly decides that at the conclusion of this class, he will retreat to the underworld and never return.

# EDUCATION, INC.

Resistance to world view change goes well beyond individual students, teachers, and programs. It emanates from the very heart of contemporary educational institutions. The intense capitalism of the late twentieth century has deeply scarred the very purpose of education. Students have become clients; teachers have become disposable assembly line workers; administrators have become corporate managers rather than educational leaders.

Not long ago, university presidents, as the educational leaders of their institutions, influenced social policy and thinking regionally and sometimes nationally. Deans and department chairs were the educational leaders of their disciplines. Emile Durkheim, as the chair of the education department at the Sorbonne, influenced French education in ways that are still evident today. Increasingly, contemporary university presidents are CEOs whose main function is fundraising; legions of vice presidents guide university financial affairs and public relations; deans have become budget and sales managers; and department chairs have become floor managers specializing in employee and consumer relations.

As a result, contemporary education is mired in the muck of consumerism. Education attempts to emulate business practices by catering to client whim in order to boost enrollments and increase "profits." The problem that is never addressed is that education has essential differences from a standard business. In most businesses, once clients plunk down their money, their obligation is fulfilled. After a product is purchased, the total pressure is on the product to perform up to the client's expectations. The client is off the hook. If the hamburger is cold, it is replaced; if the garment seam is not stitched properly, the garment is returned; if the car doesn't work, it is repaired. There are, in fact, universities attempting to emulate this model by issuing guarantees on its graduates, ensuring that if future employers find their graduates defective, they will be "repaired" at no additional charge.

Of course, the problem with treating education as a business is that in education, once "clients" plunks down their money, their obligation *begins*. Education actually has some striking similarities to a health club membership. Once health club clients pay the membership fee, they receive no benefit at all unless they make use of the facilities to exercise. Yet even here, health club client expectations are different from education "client" expectations:

- Exercisers do not expect benefit from exercise they did twenty years earlier, yet universities routinely grant credit for past coursework. Granting credit for past coursework is a marketing incentive, not an educational decision.
- Exercisers understand that they lose something when they miss an exercise session, yet students who miss classes routinely say, "I didn't miss anything, did I?" Many students don't expect or want much "education" for their money.
- Exercisers do not expect their trainers to make the recommended exercise regime easier, yet university professors are often implored to reduce course coverage and assign less work because "we are busy people who don't have time to do all this." At the pre-university level, teachers are implored by parents to give less homework because their children are busy with sports and work. Most students do not demand much educational substance as long as they are happy with the way they are treated.

- Exercisers view even the monotony of repetitive exercise as integral to their physical fitness goals, yet many students view their education as meaningless hoops they need to jump through to attain credentials to pursue a goal for which they already feel adequately prepared.
- Exercisers know that cutting exercise time or intensity means that they will receive less of a benefit; many students do not know this.
- Exercisers do not need to receive A's to verify that they have exercised; many students require A's as evidence of their very existence.
- Exercisers understand that physical health requires regular exercise over an extended period of time; many students believe they can take a large number of classes in a short period of time without missing any of their value.
- Health clubs do not need to utilize football teams, clubs, sororities, and fraternities to entice members to join; most universities do.

Though the preceding may appear to be a harsh critique of students, it is intended to be a harsh critique of what our "client-oriented" educational system has allowed students to become. Students always live up to our expectations. For fear of losing a paying student to another institution (for universities as well as the free-market public schools), we continue to lower expectations. In short, with a health club membership, most exercisers insist on working hard to gain a full benefit. Those who do not simply fade away without blaming the health club if they remain physically unfit. There are no shortcuts; one exercises or one does not. This is not true in education, a field in which schools work hard to sell the idea that learning can be easy, painless, and convenient.

Contemporary education collectively hyperventilates whenever a student is critical about anything. It is important that students feel good about the product. Faculty course evaluations are essentially customer satisfaction indicators rather than valid critiques. Don't be too tough on students, assign everyone high grades, make them feel good about themselves, and you will receive rave reviews every time. Assign a lot of work, force students to think and reflect, evaluate assignments critically, and assign the grades that the work deserves, and it is likely that you will be eaten alive on your reviews. I do wish to add the caution that, occasionally, poor teachers will use the above argument to explain their poor reviews. Yet sometimes a cigar is just a cigar, and sometimes a poor review means that someone is just a poor teacher. The problem, of course, is that under the current system, it is difficult to differentiate between the two scenarios.

Contemporary education attempts to avoid causing any discomfort to anyone, even though discomfort plays an extremely valuable role in the silent curriculum. Because students see themselves as consumer–clients, they tend to feel that frustrations of any sort are "unacceptable." (I have personally heard that word come from students in a variety of circumstances.) *Unacceptable.* It is a word one might use to describe a flawed sales transaction, and that is exactly how it is viewed. This is a micro version of the larger societal belief that nothing bad should happen to us under any circumstance; this belief is currently amplified in educational settings.

What is lost in this thinking is the role that discomfort (and even suffering) play in forcing change. We tend not to discard old views unless they are causing us some discomfort; when we are comfortable, we tend to cling to our comfort. But it is discomfort that causes change and growth. We do little of either when we are self-satisfied. It is the job of education to provide the grain of sand to students' oysters and to vicariously produce spectacular pearls.

> We should add to these sources of resistance the current mood of vocationalism and consumerism among students in the professional schools—so easily translatable into a thirst for the "hard skills" embodied in sophisticated techniques. This mood is also likely to make students resistant to the demands of any reflection on practice that does not promise immediate practical utility.[3]

Education, Inc. has also been fueled by student vocationalism and postmodern equalitarianism. Vocationalism has fueled the growth of professional programs and has created an influx of students seeking credentials rather than education. Postmodern equalitarianism has led students to view themselves as the equals of their teachers and to believe themselves capable of judging what elements are necessary in their educations. Thus, consumerism influences not only the delivery but also the substance of an education.

> "Well, are we equals?" he asked.
> "Of course we're equals," I said.
> "No," he said calmly, "we are not."

"Why, certainly we are," I protested.
"No," he said in a soft voice. "We are not equals. I am a hunter and a war-rior, and you are a pimp." [4]

Donald Schön speaks to the importance of both of these issues: vocation-alism and equalitarianism. Inherent in the educational process is the reality that because students cannot understand what it is that they need to learn, stu-dents must trust their teachers to guide them through the process. But the contemporary constrictions ensure that students who don't understand what is needed are constantly pulling in a different direction than the teachers who do know what is needed. And although students are certainly their teachers' equals in terms of basic humanity, they are not their equals in specific pro-fessional terms. The assumption of equality does not translate into a trust that teachers can use to guide students into the unknown—I do not wish to go whitewater rafting with a guide who knows as little about it as I do.

Another disturbing aspect of Education, Inc. is the growing prevalence of fast-food, drive-through education. Because consumers lead busy lives, businesses have created speedy solutions to assist their hasty consump-tion. Although "fast" works for many things, it doesn't work well with ed-ucation. Here we confront another reason why institutions will be reluc-tant to accept the reality of the silent curriculum. As most universities are attempting to reduce the amount of time it takes for a student to receive a degree or certification, the time to change a world view is increasingly squeezed out of programs. Schools legitimize the fast track by "research-ing" it and asking students if they feel that the program satisfied their needs. Students tend to judge these programs in terms of having gotten what they wanted, and they tend to give the programs high marks. Schools then offer these opinion polls as "research" that supports the fact that fast track programs work. These reviews are then used to advertise the pro-gram to future students. The problem here is that *time* is one of the basic requirements of world view transformation. When there is no time, there is no opportunity for transformation. When there is no transformation, there is no education.

The master always left you to grow at your own pace. He was never known to "push." He explained this with the following parable:
    "A man once saw a butterfly struggling to emerge from its cocoon, too slowly for his taste, so he began to blow on it gently. The warmth of his

breath speeded up the process all right. But what emerged was not a butter-
fly but a creature with mangled wings.

"In growth," the Master concluded, "you cannot speed the process up. All
you can do is abort it."[5]

The last meeting of my doctoral cohort included a luncheon where students gave testimonials about what the program meant to them and how it
changed their lives. Most of the testimonials (including mine) were predictable and forgettable. One, however, made an impression on me then
and has stuck with me over the years. One student said, "I am grateful that
this program gave me what I needed instead of what I wanted." Unfortu-
nately, consumerism has the insidious effect of giving students what they
want instead of what they need. This practice seriously erodes the goals of
any silent curriculum.

## POLITICAL RESISTANCE

We have examined world view change resistance from the frames of the individual to that of the larger institution. Now we move to the encompassing
political frame. Educational policy in this country is not made by educators.
It is made by politicians, sometimes incredibly ignorant politicians seeking
the spotlight and sometimes by incredibly intelligent politicians with clever
political and economic agendas.

Imagine that the nation's governors have been invited to a summit to discuss the future of American business: the proper role of technology in the
workplace, what can be done to improve the way companies are managed—
that sort of thing. Because politicians may have limited familiarity with
such matters, however, each governor has been invited to bring along one
advisor: a school teacher.

The idea would strike most of us as absurd. In fact, it seems exactly as
absurd as a summit on education in which each governor was accompanied
by a corporate executive. The only difference between these two absurd scenarios is that the latter actually happened. In March 1996, a conservative
Republican governor (Tommy Thompson of Wisconsin) joined IBM in
hosting the Education Summit at the company's suburban New York head-
quarters. There, various corporate chieftains joined most of the nation's

governors in issuing proclamations about the need for "higher standards" and, to no one's surprise, the importance of technology in schools.[6]

Politicians tend to loathe complexity; it doesn't work well for TV sound bites. So politicians routinely try to distill the complex teaching and learning process into simple, flawless, measurable, teacher-proof techniques; their hope is to reduce this complexity into units that can be easily assessed by standardized tests. By doing so, learning can be assigned a number and can be rank-ordered against other learning so politicians can appear to be impacting education by pointing fingers at certain schools and teachers. Politicians give this practice of measuring oversimplification the spin name "accountability." Anyone desiring an in-depth view of this topic is advised to read the latest publications of Alfie Kohn.

The problem is that thinking is messy, and deep thinking is really messy. The standards movement attempts to break an education up into isolated skills and forgettable facts. It is easier to test discrete skills and facts than it is to evaluate deep thinking. We end up with a situation in which the tail is wagging the dog. We wish to make teachers and schools accountable; we can't test the deep thinking because it is too messy; so we change the purpose of education into something that can be tested so we can test it. We then end up with a way to rank-order schools so politicians can say that one school is better than another at teaching students to pass the test.

What is lost here once again is the silent curriculum. The details of the standards are simply a gateway to the important learning to which no one is paying the slightest attention. It is like the point I used to make when teaching programming students about taking care in using real (decimal) numbers. We would take a 1 and divide it by 3. The result was .333333333333333 (extending as far out as the particular programming language allowed). We would then shorten it to .333 for purposes of the example, noting that this already distorted the value. Then we would take the .333 and multiply it by 3. When the product was .999, the question would be, "how we could get back the missing .001"? The answer was that it is gone forever. When we break knowledge into so many discrete standards and give no thought to the larger picture, we always come up .001 short.

Perhaps we need to rethink the goals and practice of professional education. We may need to reexamine the notion that the explicit curriculum is of primary importance and that all worthy students naturally grasp the silent curriculum on their own while poor students do not. We may wish to find ways to better connect our explicit curriculum to the silent curriculum. The silent knowledge perspective requires us to consider not only the explicit curriculum but also the context of a profession, a program, and a school. It also requires us to examine the manner in which that context is transmitted. Ignoring the context of the silent curriculum leads to a misunderstanding of the particular professional training.

Rigid preoccupation with an explicit curriculum often results in "weed-out" courses. My own difficulty with assembly language made me a pariah in the eyes of Dr. Irving. However, with a little more time, I became very adept with assembly language in particular and computers in general. I worked hard at it; I worked the problems and wrote the programs; I put in the time. I eventually "got it." Many of those who do not "get it" are simply discarded or simply quit too soon. An explicit curriculum can adjust for the students who get a late start. To a certain extent, the case study program adjusts for these students. The CIS department chair acknowledged that students arriving with a strong background often become bored with the program (which moves slowly at the beginning), as most students enter the program without that strong background. Even in this program, however, some students are not prepared for the sudden intensity of the programming sequence. Certainly some students simply need more time to allow them to master the assigned programming tasks. Each professional program needs to examine students for promise and to set up additional learning experiences to help students meet required milestones.

I believe that students as well as teachers could benefit from an understanding of the existence and workings of a silent curriculum. It is one thing to tell students to do something because it is important; it is quite another to explain to them *why* it is important. There is value in explaining to students the nature of ritual and myth and how vital learning is indirectly transmitted through them. Making explicit the workings of the silent curriculum could also work to overcome many of the resistances cited earlier; in our modern culture, we view education as we do because that is what we have been taught. It is time for us all to learn what can't be taught.

# NOTES

1. Donald A. Schön, *Educating the Reflective Practitioner: Toward a New Design in Teaching and Learning in the Professions* (San Francisco, Calif.: Jossey-Bass, 1987), 313.

2. Erving Goffman, "On Cooling the Mark Out: Some Aspects of Adaptation to Failure," *Psychiatry: Journal for the Study of Interpersonal Relations* 15, no. 4 (1952): 462.

3. Schön, *Educating,* 313.

4. Carlos Castaneda, *Journey to Ixtlan: The Lessons of Don Juan* (New York: Pocket Books, 1974), 57.

5. Anthony de Mello, *One Minute Wisdom* (New York: Doubleday, 1988), 167.

6. Alfie Kohn, "Introduction: The Five Hundred Pound Gorilla," in *Education, Inc.: Turning Learning into a Business*, ed. Alfie Kohn (Arlington Heights, Ill.: IRI Skylight Training and Publishing, 1997), v.

# Bibliography

Anderson, Walter Truett. "Four Different Ways to Be Absolutely Right." In *The Truth about the Truth*, ed. Walter Truett Anderson, 110–116. New York: Tarcher Putnam, 1995.

——. "Introduction: What's Going on Here." In *The Truth about the Truth*, ed. Walter Truett Anderson, 1–11. New York: Tarcher Putnam, 1995.

Barnett, Lincoln. *The Universe and Dr. Einstein.* 2d rev. ed., with a foreword by Albert Einstein. New York: Bantam, 1978.

Berger, Peter L., and Thomas Luckmann. *The Social Construction of Reality: A Treatise in the Sociology of Knowledge.* 1966. Reprint, New York: Anchor Books, 1989.

Berman, Sanford. "Cataloging Castaneda." In *The Don Juan Papers: Further Castaneda Controversies*, ed. Richard de Mille, 100–103. Belmont, Calif.: Wadsworth Publishing, 1990.

Brookes, Michael Lewes. "Quantum Foam." *New Scientist* 28, no. 2191 (19 June 1999): 1–4. http://www.ldolphin.org/qfoam.html (accessed 23 May 2001).

Brown, Julian. *Minds, Machines, and the Multiverse: The Quest for the Quantum Computer.* New York: Simon & Schuster, 2000.

Campbell, J. *Understanding John Dewey.* Chicago: Open Court, 1995.

Canter, Lee. "Let the Educator Beware: A Response to Curwin and Mendler." *Educational Leadership* 46, no. 2 (October 1988): 71–73.

Canter, Lee, and Marlene Canter. *Assertive Discipline: Positive Behavior Management for Today's Classroom.* Santa Monica, Calif.: Lee Canter and Associates, 1992.

Capra, Fritjof. *The Tao of Physics: An Exploration of the Parallels between Modern Physics and Eastern Mysticism.* 1975. Reprint, Boston: Shambala, 1985.

Castaneda, Carlos. *The Teachings of Don Juan: A Yaqui Way of Knowledge.* New York: Ballantine Books, 1968.

———. *The Teachings of Don Juan: A Yaqui Way of Knowledge.* 1968. Thirtieth Anniversary Edition, New York: Washington Square Press, 1998.

———. *Journey to Ixtlan: The Lessons of Don Juan.* New York: Pocket Books, 1974.

———. *Tales of Power.* New York: Pocket Books, 1976.

———. *The Second Ring of Power.* New York: Simon and Schuster, 1977.

———. *The Eagle's Gift.* New York: Simon and Schuster, 1981.

———. *The Fire from Within.* New York: Pocket Books, 1984.

———. *The Power of Silence: Further Lessons of Don Juan.* New York: Simon and Schuster, 1987.

———. *The Art of Dreaming.* New York: Harper Perennial, 1994.

———. *Active Side of Infinity.* New York: Harper Perennial, 2000.

Castaneda, Margaret Runyan. *A Magical Journey with Carlos Castaneda.* Victoria, Canada: Millennia Press, 1997.

Chopra, Deepak. *The Seven Spiritual Laws of Success: A Practical Guide to the Fulfillment of Your Dreams.* San Rafael, Calif.: New World Library, 1994.

Collins, Randall. *Three Sociological Traditions.* New York: Oxford University Press, 1985.

de Mello, Anthony. *One Minute Wisdom.* New York: Doubleday, 1988.

de Mille, Richard. "The Art of Stalking Castaneda." In *The Don Juan Papers: Further Castaneda Controversies*, ed. Richard de Mille, 9–13. Belmont, Calif.: Wadsworth Publishing, 1990.

———. "The Shaman of Academe." In *The Don Juan Papers: Further Castaneda Controversies*, ed. Richard de Mille, 17–23. Belmont, Calif.: Wadsworth Publishing, 1990.

———. "Validity Is Not Authenticity." In *The Don Juan Papers: Further Castaneda Controversies*, ed. Richard de Mille, 39–67. Belmont, Calif.: Wadsworth Publishing, 1990.

Deutsch, David, and Michael Lockwood. "The Quantum Physics of Time Travel." *Scientific American* 270, no. 3 (March 1994): 68–74.

Douglas, Mary. *How Institutions Think.* Syracuse, New York: Syracuse University Press, 1986.

———. "The Authenticity of Castaneda." In *Implicit Meanings: Essays in Anthropology*, ed. Mary Douglas, 193–200. London: Routledge, 1993.

Durkheim, Emile. *The Elementary Forms of the Religious Life.* 1915. Reprint, New York: Free Press, 1965.

———. *The Division of Labor in Society.* Trans. George Simpson. 1893. Reprint, New York: Free Press, 1933.

———. *Education and Sociology.* New York: Free Press, 1956.

———. *Professional Ethics and Civic Morals.* New York: Routledge, 1957.

———. *Moral Education: A Study in the Theory and Application of the Sociology of Education.* New York: Free Press, 1973.

Ebaugh, Helen Rose Fuchs. *Becoming An Ex: The Process of Role Exit.* Chicago: University Of Chicago Press, 1988.

Elkind, David. "School and Family in the Postmodern World." *Phi Delta Kappan* 77, no. 1 (September 1995): 8–14.

Eliade, Mircea. *Shamanism: Archaic Techniques of Ecstasy.* 1951. Reprint, New York: Princeton University Press, 1972.

———. *Rites and Symbols of Initiation: The Mysteries of Birth and Rebirth.* 1958. Reprint, New York: Harper & Row, 1975.

Fleck, Ludwig. *Genesis and Development of a Scientific Fact.* Chicago: University of Chicago Press, 1981.

Goldschmidt, Walter. Foreword to *The Teachings of Don Juan: A Yaqui Way of Knowledge,* by Carlos Castaneda. New York: Ballantine Books, 1968.

Goldstein, Martin, and Inge F. Goldstein. *How We Know: An Exploration of the Scientific Process.* New York: Plenum, 1978.

Goffman, Erving. "On Cooling the Mark Out: Some Aspects of Adaptation to Failure." *Psychiatry: Journal for the Study of Interpersonal Relations* 15, no. 4 (1952), 451–463.

———. *The Presentation of Self in Everyday Life.* Garden City, New York: Doubleday, 1959.

———. *Interaction Ritual: Essays in Face-to-Face Behavior.* Chicago: Adline, 1967.

———. *Frame Analysis: An Essay on the Organization of Experience.* Boston: Northeast University Press, 1974.

Goodman, Nelson. *Ways of Worldmaking.* Indianapolis, Ind.: Hackett, 1978.

Goulet, Jean-Guy. "Dreams and Visions in Other Lifeworlds." In *Being Changed: The Anthropology of Extraordinary Experience,* ed. David. E. Young and Jean-Guy Goulet, 16–38. Ontario, Canada: Broadview Press, 1994.

Gribbin, John. *In Search of Schrödinger's Cat: Quantum Physics and Reality.* New York: Bantam, 1984.

Guédon, Marie Francoise. "Dene Ways and the Ethnographer's Culture." In *Being Changed: The Anthropology of Extraordinary Experience,* ed. David. E. Young and Jean-Guy Goulet, 39–70. Ontario, Canada: Broadview Press, 1994.

Harner, Michael. *The Way of the Shaman.* New York: Harper & Row, 1990.

Hoyningen-Huene, Paul. *Reconstructing Scientific Revolutions: Thomas S. Kuhn's Philosophy of Science.* Chicago: University of Chicago Press, 1993.

Kalweit, Holger. *Shamans, Healers, and Medicine Men.* Boston: Shambala, 1992.

——. *Dreamtime and Inner Space: The World of the Shaman.* Boston: Shambala, 1998.

King, Stephen. *On Writing: A Memoir of the Craft.* New York: Pocket Books, 2000.

Kohn, Alfie. "Introduction: The Five Hundred Pound Gorilla." In *Education, Inc.: Turning Learning into a Business*, ed. Alfie Kohn, v–xxii. Arlington Heights, Ill.: IRI Skylight Training and Publishing, 1997.

Kuhn, Thomas S. *The Structure of Scientific Revolutions.* 2d ed., Chicago: University of Chicago Press, 1970.

Lévi-Strauss, Claude. *Structural Anthropology.* New York: Basic Books, 1963.

——. *Myth and Meaning: Cracking the Code of Culture.* 1978. Reprint, New York: Schocken Books, 1995.

Lincoln, Bruce. *Discourse and the Construction of Society: Comparative Studies of Myth, Ritual, and Classification.* New York: Oxford University Press, 1989.

Manning, Philip. *Erving Goffman and Modern Sociology.* Stanford, Calif.: Stanford University Press, 1992.

Markoff, John. "Quantum Computing Is Becoming More than Just a Good Idea." *New York Times on the Web.* http://www.nytimes.com, (28 April 1998). (Accessed 23 May 2001).

Marton, Yves. "The Experiential Approach to Anthropology and Castaneda's Ambiguous Legacy." In *Being Changed: The Anthropology of Extraordinary Experience*, ed. David. E. Young and Jean-Guy Goulet, 273–287. Ontario, Canada: Broadview Press, 1994.

McDermott, Richard. "Reasons, Rules, and the Ring of Experience: Reading Our World into Carlos Castaneda's Works." *Human Studies* 2, no. 1 (January 1979): 31–46.

McLaren, Peter. *Schooling as a Ritual Performance: Toward a Political Economy of Educational Symbols and Gestures.* New York: Routledge, 1993.

Murray, Stephen O. "The Invisibility of Scientific Scorn." In *The Don Juan Papers: Further Castaneda Controversies*, ed. Richard de Mille, 198–202. Belmont, Calif.: Wadsworth Publishing, 1990.

Oakes, Guy. *The Soul of the Salesman: The Moral Ethos of Personal Sales.* Atlantic Highlands, N.J.: Humanities Press International, 1990.

Peach, Filiz. "David Deutsch Interviewed by Filiz Peach." *Philosophy Now* 30 (December/January 2000): 24.

Reno, Stephen J. "If Don Juan Did Not Exist, It Would Be Necessary to Invent Him." In *The Don Juan Papers: Further Castaneda Controversies*, ed. Richard de Mille, 254–258. Belmont, Calif.: Wadsworth Publishing, 1990.

Riesman, Paul. "Fictions of Art and Science, or Does It Matter whether Don Juan Really Exists?" In *The Don Juan Papers: Further Castaneda Contro-*

*versies*, edited by Richard de Mille, 207–216. Belmont, Calif.: Wadsworth Publishing, 1990.

Rigoni, David P., and Donald R. LaMagdeleine. "Computer Majors' Education as Moral Enterprise: A Durkheimian Analysis." *Journal of Moral Education* 27, no. 4 (December 1998): 489–503.

Rosenau, Pauline Marie. *Post-Modernism and the Social Sciences: Insights, Inroads, and Intrusions*. Princeton, N.J.: Princeton University Press, 1992.

Schank, Roger C. *Tell Me a Story*. Evanston, Ill.: Northwestern University Press, 1990.

Schein, Edgar. *Professional Education*. New York: McGraw-Hill, 1973.

Schein, Edgar H. *Organizational Culture and Leadership*. San Francisco, Calif.: Jossey-Bass, 1985.

———. "What Is Culture?" In *Reframing Organizational Culture*, ed. Peter J. Frost, Larry F. Moore, Meryl Reis Lewis, Craig C. Lundberg, and Joanne Martin, 234–253. Newbury Park, Calif.: Sage Publications, 1991.

Schön, Donald A. *The Reflective Practitioner: How Professionals Think in Action*. San Francisco, Calif.: Basic Books, 1983.

———. *Educating the Reflective Practitioner: Toward a New Design in Teaching and Learning in the Professions*. San Francisco, Calif.: Jossey-Bass, 1987.

Sebald, Hans. "Roasting Rabbits in Tularemia, or the Lion, the Witch, and the Horned Toad." In *The Don Juan Papers: Further Castaneda Controversies*, ed. Richard de Mille, 34–38. Belmont, Calif.: Wadsworth Publishing, 1990.

Silva, Ramón Medina. "Almost We Cannot Speak about It." In *The Don Juan Papers: Further Castaneda Controversies*, ed. Richard de Mille, 334–335. Belmont, Calif.: Wadsworth Publishing, 1990.

Spoto, Donald. *The Hidden Jesus: A New Life*. New York: St. Martin's Press, 1998.

Swartz, Lise. "Being Changed by Cross-Cultural Encounters." In *Being Changed: The Anthropology of Extraordinary Experience*, ed. David. E. Young and Jean-Guy Goulet, 209–236. Ontario, Canada: Broadview Press, 1994.

Traweek, Sharon. *Beamtimes and Lifetimes: The World of High Energy Physicists*. Cambridge: Harvard University Press, 1988.

van de Wetering, Janwillem. *A Glimpse of Nothingness: Experiences in an American Zen Community*. New York: Washington Square Press, 1975.

Wilson, C. Roderick. "Seeing They See Not." In *Being Changed: The Anthropology of Extraordinary Experience*, ed. David. E. Young and Jean-Guy Goulet, 197–208. Ontario, Canada: Broadview Press, 1994.

Wilson, James Q. *Bureaucracy: What Government Agencies Do and Why They Do It*. New York: Basic Books, 1990.

# Index

Anderson, Walter Truett, 17, 21
attention, 49, 88–90

Berger and Luckmann, 25–27

Castaneda, Carlos, 9, 65–93, 136;
field research/methodological
secrecy, 68, 71–73; going native
[cognicentrism], 71, 77–78; words
of other writers, 68, 74; writings as
fiction, 68, 71–72, 78, 79
Castaneda, Margaret Runyon, 72–78;
cognicentrism, 74–75, 77–78;
ethnographic research, 74, 76–77;
The Great Fear, 75–76
cognicentrism, 74–78
Collins, Randall, 58–59, 89
connectedness, 33–36, 39

de Mello, Anthony, 145, 150
de Mille, Richard, 68, 70–74
Deutsch, David, 34–35, 37
Don Juan, 1, 9, 65, 67, 73, 75–76,
78–95; focusing attention, 88–89;
loss/suffering, 93–94, 136; silent
knowledge, 84, 88–89, 96, 148,
162; tricking/pseudotasks, 87–89;

warrior, 81, 83; warrior vs. ordinary,
78, 86–87, 91, 94, 118, 129
Douglas, Mary, 60, 62, 70
Durkheim, Emile, 53–58, 62, 65, 155;
myth and ritual, 53–56, 89–92, 139;
sacred and profane, 81, 117–119

Education, Inc., 155–160;
client/consumerism, 156–157, 160;
health club analogy, 156–157;
political resistance, 160–162;
reducing time, 159;
vocationalism/egalitarianism,
158–159
Einstein, Albert, 29-33, 37; General
Relativity, 30, 32, 34; photoelectric
effect, 29; Special Relativity, 30–32;
Unified Field Theory, 33, 37
Eliade, Mircea, 72, 81, 83, 92
Elkind, David, 20
explicit/formal curriculum, 104,
108–109, 112, 139, 142, 147,
151–153, 161–162

Garfinkel, Harold, 59, 67
Goffman, Erving, 58–60, 62, 71, 90,
117, 126, 151

104–106, 116, 129, 139–140; not
asking for help, 140–141; play, 127,
140–141; problem solving, 104,
106–108, 116, 129–136, 139;
problem solving antithesis, 135;
suffering/discomfort and
loss/renewal, 48, 50, 136–138, 145;
time/work, 107, 126–127, 140, 145,
148–149, 159; trickery, 101, 114,
146
silent knowledge, 84, 89, 96, 101,
127–128, 142
sorcerer/sorcery, 79–83, 88
Spoto, Donald, 23

theory, 11, 13–16, 20
Traweek, Sharon, 49, 117, 125–126,
132–133
truth, 22–24, 82

urinal game, 56–58

van de Wetering, Janwillem, 101, 124,
128

what I learned, 62–63
world view [professional], 54, 88,
111–112, 118, 124
world views, 16–17, 24, 66, 91, 143,
145–150; hybrid paradigms,
20–24; major Western world views,
*18;* modernist/techno-rational, 10,
24, 42–44; premodern, modern,
postmodern, hybrid, 17–24
world view transformation, 42, 65, 67,
95, 146; approached indirectly, 51;
resistance and loss, 50; risk, 50,
145; time, 51–52, 145, 159
worldmaking, 24, 26–27, 38, 62, 124

# About the Author

**David Rigoni** has been involved in teaching his whole life. He taught high school English in both public and private schools. After suffering a "massive compositional infarction" (total burnout from evaluating writing assignments), he realized he needed a change. So, he explored the emerging computer field (microcomputers had just been born), enrolled in courses, and shortly moved to teaching in a university Computer Information Systems department. One day, as he was lecturing on telecommunications, he found a second mind-slice of himself thinking about vacationing in Mexico, and a third mind-slice observing this phenomenon, all without missing a beat. At this, he realized he needed another change and, when opportunities presented themselves, he assumed a series of administrative duties. He eventually chaired (not all at the same time) a Behavioral Arts and Sciences division, a Computer Information Systems department, and a Teacher Education department. He now serves in the latter role.

His academic interests include the sociology of education, systems and critical thinking, and problem solving. His nonacademic interests involve devouring vampire fiction and researching how much endurance people have for puns before turning violent.

His doctorate is in educational leadership from the University of St. Thomas in St. Paul, Minnesota. He lives with his family in the Twin Cities area.